DISCOVER CROCHET YARN ART

A COMPREHENSIVE, ILLUSTRATED BEGINNER'S GUIDE

GENEVIEVE ANN CHRISTESON

CONTENTS

INTRODUCTION

Have you ever admired the attractive, yarn-crafted projects exhibited at craft markets or the eye-catching, trendy crochet fabric designs that people wear? Maybe you wonder if you should give crochet craft a try?

Let me assure you that once you start the addictive yarn craft, you will find yourself searching for more projects to grow your crochet skills.

Crochet craft not only keeps your hands busy but is also a highly recuperative hobby that can give you hours of pleasure and plenty of much-needed quiet contemplation time. Creating unique possessions that can be worn, displayed, or given as gifts appeals to many crafters.

Moreover, the craft does not have to cost an arm and a leg while still having the potential to earn you a side income.

Think about it! What better way to earn extra cash than with unique handmade fabrics of your design?

The versatility of the crochet craft has survived hundreds of years to bring creative pleasure, mental stimulation, and an opportunity to grow self-esteem. Crochet is less physically challenging and considerably more economical than some other hobbies. The great thing about crochet is that it is a yarn craft available to people of all ages who enjoy exercising their creative skills.

Yarn craft, mainly crocheting, is a highly popular handcraft. Whether you are an experienced crafter or a novice, crochet yarn crafting is a satisfying hobby that has the potential to become a lucrative side hustle. You will learn about great business opportunities and how to recognize whether your yarn craft or crochet hobby can profit you.

If you are a creative person interested in trying your hand at the artful and highly satisfying crafting skill of crochet but don't know where to start, "Discover Crochet Yarn Art" is the right book for you. You will find plenty of helpful hints and tips for creating yarn craft adventures in the beautiful crochet world. Here, you will also discover heaps of information about the differences between knitting and crochet, as well as the positive influences of crocheting.

You will find answers to some of the most frequently asked questions, helpful resources for patterns, stitches, and ideal beginner and refresher projects to excite your creativity.

There is also plenty of information about yarn types and how to choose the best yarn for your crochet project. Finally, there are added particulars about the benefits and afford-ability of crochet compared to other hobbies.

And, if you are a left-handed crafter, there are clear, easy-to-follow instructions to help you join the popular crocheting community by designing and creating your unique projects.

In this book, the author wishes to share her knowledge and experience in yarn crafting to help you create quality, unique objects with minimal frustration. She also plans to help you learn about this delightful, relaxing art by clearly under-standing the terminology, techniques, and tools specific to the craft. You will discover plenty of helpful tips for learning to read a crochet pattern while making the best choices for selected trade instruments.

This essential yarn craft crochet manual details the skills needed by every beginner crocheter' to produce beautiful, functional, and highly original works of art. There is helpful advice from master crafters, with plenty of experience in crochet craft, on where to source free patterns and how to make the basic stitches. You will also learn the importance of choosing the best stitch for specific projects and how these stitches can be used to create unique, one-of-a-kind designs. Finally, the helpful hacks for avoiding costly mistakes will ensure you make better choices, for crochet projects of which you can be very proud.

The crochet glossary offers plenty of information for newbie crocheters to discover the meanings of crochet terms and instructions.

Genevieve Ann Christeson has been passionate about yarn arts for most of her life. She began with knitting and decided to give crochet a try after watching her grandmother create a treasure trove of intricate, beautiful, and colorful pieces.

In learning crochet, it came to her attention that many people encountered similar concerns in their creative attempts.

Having been a social worker by profession, Genevieve felt it necessary to create a book that would help solve those problems and take away the frustration from what should be a beautiful, relaxing, and creative endeavor.

Genevieve has shared her love of crochet by imparting essential skills and techniques for a beginner crocheter learning the craft. There is also plenty of helpful information for crocheters at all levels of expertise. You will find various super-inspiring projects from which to choose, all of which are perfectly designed for enthusiastic beginners and crochet crafters looking to renew their love of the craft.

What's more, the information shared will create in you a passion for crochet and the sense of achievement that comes with every completed project.

Whether you are a beginner or someone who is looking for a refresher course in crochet, you will find step-by-step instructions and easy-to-follow helpful advice for getting started on gorgeous crochet projects for your home, family, and friends. With the skills you will learn in this extensive crochet book, you have the chance to create a multitude of exciting and unique crochet projects.

So, let's start learning more about the exciting and highly versatile world of crochet craft's and its many benefits!

A BRIEF HISTORY OF CROCHET AND YARN ARTS

Have you ever wondered how crochet handicrafts started and where they originated? People are inherently creative, so it may not be surprising to find out that many people have discovered innovative ways to make advantageous items for fishing, storage, warmth, and personal decoration throughout the ages.

THE ORIGINS OF CROCHET

Many different types of handwork, such as embroidery, weaving, and knitting, date back thousands of years. Although there appears to be no definitive starting point, crochet is believed to have developed during the 16th century. During that time, crochet was known as "chain lace" in England and "crochet lace" in France.

The word "crochet" has both French and Germanic roots, *croche* and *croc*, both of which mean "hook." In the 1600s, the term crocheting referred to joining pieces of lace together. However, modern crochet crafters will attest to the art of crochet being a versatile, inventive, and attractive way of creating an enormous diversity of serviceable and decorative articles.

European Beginnings

Crochet yarn craft may have begun in Europe in the 1500s, where it was known as "nun's lace" because it was worked mainly by women of the cloth for church garments and textiles.

In France, Italy, Spain, and Belgium, yarn craft using a hook is called crochet. The skill is known as *virkning* in Sweden, *hekling* in Norway, *haekling* in Denmark, and *haken* in the Netherlands.

Crochet evolved from *tambouring*, using a hook to push the thread through fabric stretched over a frame.

By the end of the 18th century, the French discarded the background fabric to work stitches individually. The technique became known as "crochet in the air." Eleonore Riego de la Branchardière developed a highly desirable method known as "lace-like crochet," which she readily shared with millions of women by duplicating patterns for other yarn crafters to copy.

Amongst the first crocheted items were a variety of attractive, useful, elegant, and valuable purses.

Arabian and Eastern Influences

Crochet may have its origins in Arabia, from where it spread to the West via the Arab trade routes. Very old South American tribes used crochet adornments for young adolescents reaching puberty. Early examples of Eastern three-dimensional crochet dolls were found in China.

Irish Crochet and the Great Irish Famine

From 1845 to 1850, Ireland suffered an awful potato famine, which threw the nation into horrible poverty, forcing the population to live below the accepted standards of propriety and respectability.

Traditional Irish crochet was made using a thin steel hook and fine linen thread to create attractive separate lace motifs. Once finished, they were fastened together with picots, knots, and chain stitches to form lovely tablecloths.

During these harsh years, people of all ages crocheted between chores to create simple items of warm clothing, washcloths, rugs, and throws. Gradually, their skills improved as they designed new patterns and sold their crafts to keep their families alive. As a result, when the Irish immigrants arrived in America during the early 1900s, their yarn craft skills were much admired, and they instantly found success among their new neighbors.

English Crochet Heritage

During the 16th century, European royals adorned themselves with magnificent lace gowns, exotic lacy trimmings, and headpieces. It is thought that the poorer classes mimicked these fancy and expensive garments and ornamentations by making crocheted items. Thus, crochet garnered a reputation for being an inferior craft until Queen Victoria gave her regal seal of acceptance to the beautiful lace pieces crafted by Irish women struggling to survive during the great famine. The queen also mastered the skill of crochet and is believed to have thoroughly enjoyed making scarves for war veterans. By the end of Queen Victoria's reign, many English women were hooked entirely on crochet's new and highly prized yarn art.

Crochet During the Early 1900s

In the early 1900s, Walter Edmund Roth discovered the Guyana Indigenous tribes used crocheted articles for adornment, tiny dolls, fringes, and ponchos.

Crochet gradually moved from utility items to more decorative fashion pieces such as the cloche hat and magnificently crafted evening gowns that echoed popular designs of the period.

The War Years

During World War I and II crochet gained dominance as British and U.S. women of all ages began designing and creating useful clothing items from wool scraps, to contribute to the war effort. Trench caps and snug ear warmers made their debut for the troops. In addition, many needle-crafted articles—sewn, knitted, quilted, and crocheted—were made for the wounded, asylum-seekers, fugitives, or exiles during the war years. These items helped boost morale for the thousands of people on the home front. Crochet was also used during the war to mend garments, as they were too expensive to replace.

The 1950s to 1970s

The post-war years saw hand-crafted crochet designs flourish to become an integral part of fashion. Designer dresses, jackets, skirts, and evening wear became the rage and were chosen above the mass-produced machine-made clothing of the day.

Crochet boomed during these decades. The granny square became one of the most popular designs of the era and was used for jackets, rugs, and many other exciting articles. Designs became more colorful and exotic. The variety of crochet items was endless, from attractive crocheted mini-dresses, dainty bikinis, and bright waistcoats to cushions, curtains, and floor coverings.

From the 1980s to the 1990s

Crochet gathered momentum as people worldwide discovered the versatility of the yarn craft as classic hats, designer scarves, lovely doilies, and tablecloths made their debut.

In 1994, "crochet queen" Gwen Blakley Kinsler encouraged people to take up crochet as a worthwhile, relaxing, and highly creative hobby. As a result, she founded the Crochet Guild of America, which is still functional and actively supports crochet crafters worldwide.

Crafted Items

In ancient times, most items made from yarn were made for practical purposes. For example, anglers and hunters knotted strands of woven fibers, strips of cloth, or cords to trap animals and snare birds and fish. Gradually, people added fishing nets and baskets to their repertoire of valued items.

After that, yarn craft expanded to include personal embellishments and decorations for special occasions, including religious rites and community celebrations. People also used crochet items for decorative arm and neck bands, along with ankle and wrist straps.

In Victorian times, crocheted items became the rage for lamp covers, mats, tablecloths, and antimacassars used to protect chair backs from hair oil. There were also purses, birdcage covers, tobacco pouches, caps, waistcoats, and knee rugs.

From 1900 to 1930, many women crocheted slumber rugs, sleigh rugs, hot water bottle covers, cushions, and tea and coffeepot cozies. Potholders also made their debut during these years.

During the 1960s and 1970s, crochet projects developed as a fundamental and exciting new means of free-form expression, depicting fascinating abstract designs that are still seen in many twenty-first-century crochet projects.

Crochet Today

Over the years, crochet has been constantly revived and improved. Great designers like Dolce & Gabbana and Dior continue to feature gorgeous crochet creations from time to time. In addition, thanks to the emergence of social media, crochet crafts have grown in popularity, causing the formation and establishment of many crochet communities and blogs.

So, if you are ready to plunge into the amazingly creative and potentially lucrative world of crochet, here is your chance to learn more about this fascinating yarn craft.

TOOLS AND MATERIALS

Interestingly, different yarn crafts have developed intriguing names over time. Among these are Tunisian crochet, needle lace, knotless netting to macramé, shepherd's knitting, and naalebinding, to name but a few.

Crochet Materials

The most common materials considered suitable for crochet crafts included cotton, linen, or hemp thread and spool yarn. In addition, silk, chenille, wool yarns, and silver and gold threads were used for colorwork and additional glamour.

Throughout the ages, a variety of materials have been used for each yarn craft type, including human and animal hair, flax, hemp, and various grasses.

Gradually, cotton thread, wool, silk, linen thread, and mohair became popular choices. Today there is an added variety of exciting novelty mixtures, metal thread, and different types and thicknesses of string and synthetic yarns. Scraps of fabric, unspun wool, and plastic can be fashioned into any number of beautiful objects.

Modern crochet crafters can select steel, plastic, or aluminum hooks from various available sizes purchased from department stores, craft shops or secured online.

In earlier times, however, people probably used finger crochet before experimenting with fish and animal bones, horns, combs, spoons, and suitable wood pieces. Then, during the great Irish famine, it is believed that someone began to crochet using a small hook fashioned from a needle or stiff wire inserted into a cork for easier handling.

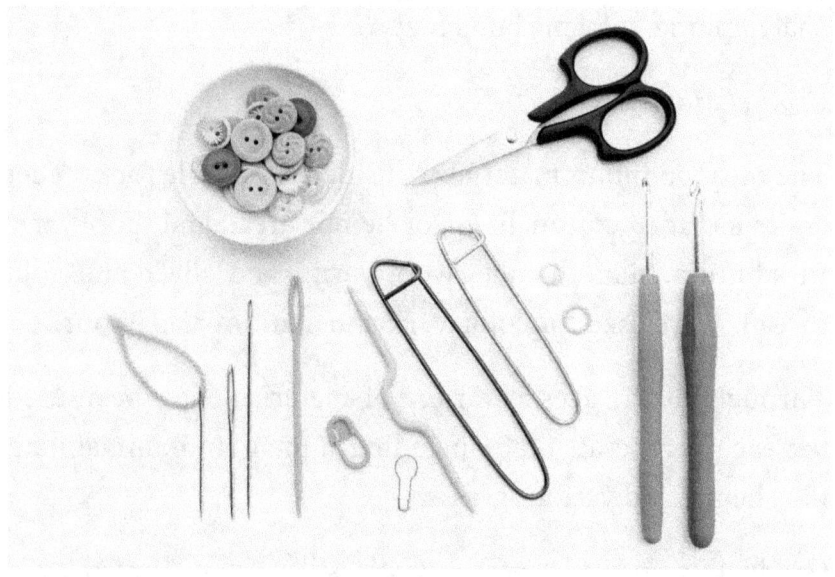

MODERN AND YESTERYEAR TECHNIQUES

It's interesting to discover the change in crochet techniques and methods. Let's look at some of these methods and how they evolved into today's familiar crochet techniques.

Holding the Yarn

Every crochet crafter has a unique way of controlling their yarn despite crochet methods having changed significantly over the years. At first, during the early 1800s, the hook and yarn were supported in the crafter's right hand and lifted over the crochet hook with the right forefinger. Then, towards the middle of the 1800's, the thread was held in the left hand, as most right-handed crochet crafters do today.

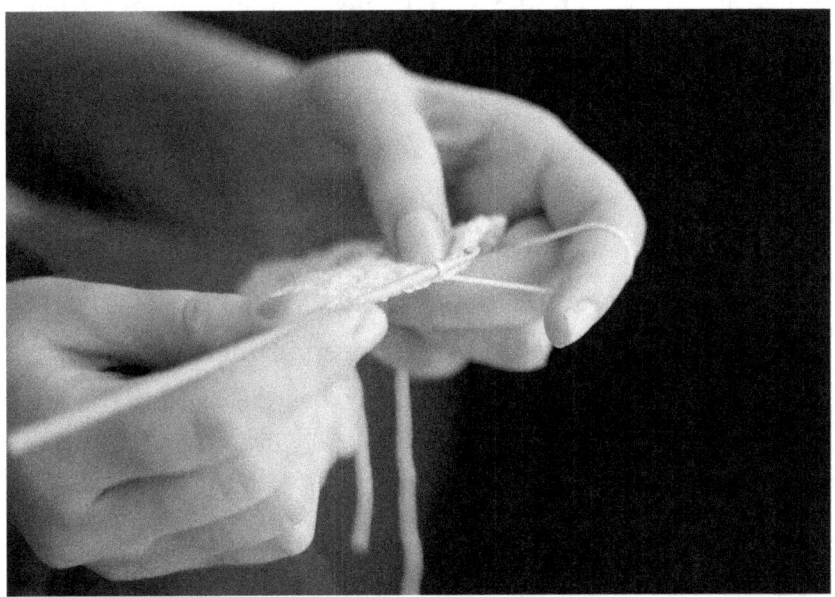

Working Rows

Some crochet crafters believed that the crochet project's tension should be kept the same to avoid unsightly work. In addition, joining yarn at the start of each new row improves the finish.

Fortunately, modern pattern instructions usually direct the crocheter to work in both the front and back faces of the crochet article, which lends the entire crocheting process greater versatility and makes it easier to accomplish an attractive finished project.

For example, patterns dating back to the 1800's instructed the crafter to push the crochet hook through the back half of each stitch, which was considered ideal for table runners. However, most modern patterns using single crochet stitches insert the hook through both loops, making thicker, more substantial articles such as slipper soles and carry bags.

CROCHET PATTERNS

Written patterns came into existence around the 1800's. The first patterns are believed to have been printed in 1824 when people began to write down their designs in a structured form. Before that date, most people copied other crafters' work.

In some cases, samplers were used to display stitches. These samplers were often sewn onto pieces of fabric and kept safe for future reference. Sometimes, a bar sampler depicting various stitches was made into a long strip.

Then, during the early 1900's, crafters could buy tiny pattern samples attached to their choice of yarn. One of the earliest patterns was a colored crocheted filigree purse. Sadly, many early crochet patterns were not accurate, so crochet crafters often preferred to use illustrations as their guide.

Crochet Books

It may surprise you to learn that crochet books have been available for many years. These works are often translated into different languages, which have helped spread the exciting skill of crochet craft worldwide.

Yarn crafters interested in crochet discovered crochet books in several countries. Eleonore Riego de la Branchardiere was one of the most famous French crochet experts. She published more than 100 books about crochet and early yarn craft. These books have been translated into many different languages worldwide.

Most early crochet books were small, measuring four by six inches, with beautiful woodcut illustrations. Each tiny book was a treasure trove filled with intricate patterns for dainty lace collars or decorative cuffs. There were also instructions for slippers, socks, and caps.

HISTORY OF KNITTING

The term "knitting" is derived from the word "knot," which means to secure the yarn to make a piece of fabric using two or more knitting needles and wool, silk, thread, or other fibers.

Knitting is believed to have originated in the Middle East, from where the craft technique spread via the trade routes to Europe and the Americas.

Ancient knitted items dating back to the 11th century CE were found in Egypt. The Spanish royal family employed Muslim weavers whose skills in crafting various things such as beautiful cushion covers and gloves made them valuable workers.

Archaeological digs led to the discovery that the knitting craft spread through Europe during the 14th century and to Britain during the 16th century. Knitted items were likely made by families as a source of income. Amongst these items, sweaters proved the most popular clothing type for the local anglers.

The Industrial Revolution

During the Industrial Revolution, the machinery employed to spin yarn, manufacture fabric, and knit lace had a substantial negative impact on hand-knitted fabric. But White Russians, who still used weaving to make various things, shared their skills with Chinese caravaners, who used camel hair to make many serviceable items.

The War Years

Knitting during the Second World War encouraged people to make practical, warm winter items for the Army and Navy. In many instances, because of the shortage of yarn during that time, people unraveled clothing items unsuitable for wear to re-knit the thread. Crochet and knitted items were handed to soldiers and sailors to help boost morale and to increase a sense of positive concern and support for the troops.

Post-War

The post-war years saw the beginning of new, exciting yarn colors and plenty of gorgeous patterns that spurred interest in the popularity of hand knitting, resulting in a knitting revival that may only be matched by modern-day interest in the yarn craft.

From the 20th Century to Modern Times

In the 1980's, cheaper woven products made their debut, forcing the hand-weaving art to decline.

Knitwear came back into fashion in the twenty-first century when handmade items became popular. As a result, exotic natural animal fibers such as alpaca, merino, and angora became the rage. In addition, plant fibers are now available in various colors and weights, less expensive than their animal counterparts.

Many crafters have participated in yarn bombing, where large pieces of knitted fabric are used to cover public objects in the form of knitted graffiti that makes a colorful statement by the crafter.

THE HISTORY OF MACRAMÉ

When you think of macramé, you may likely picture intricately woven contraptions for hanging plants and glass shelving to hold delicate ornaments. The complex, twisted, serpentine rope structures were also popular for lampshades, bags, belts and comfortable hammocks favored by people with a bohemian leaning.

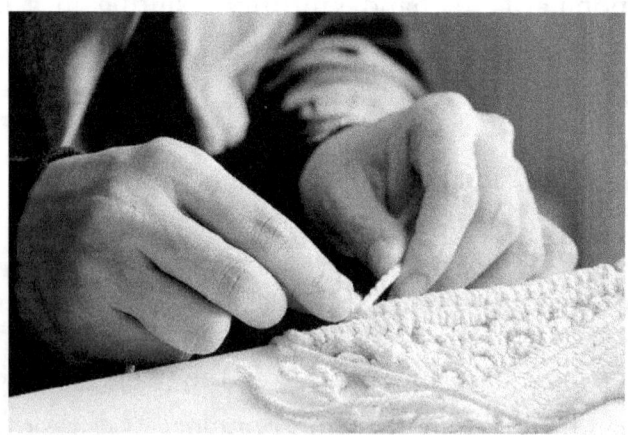

The Arab Connection

Many believe the hand-rope craft of macramé originated in Arabia, where, during the 13th century, weavers in the country tied elaborate decorative knots to secure the loose ends of woven fabrics such as shawls and towels. Thus, macramé is derived from the Arabic word *migramah*, meaning fringe.

During the 15th century, the Moors introduced the Arabic knot-tying technique to the Spanish during their occupation of Spain. Interest in macramé spread to Italy and France before the intricate knotting craft reached England, where Queen Mary II instructed her ladies-in-waiting in the art of macramé.

Victorian Power

Almost 200 years later, Queen Victoria popularized the craft, and very soon, almost everything that could be knotted was. From table linen and bedspreads to shawls, gown trims, and drapes, women of all walks of life took up macramé as one of their favorite hobbies.

The Maritime Connection

Although modern macramé is often favored by women, many years ago, sailors used their knotting skills to create some of the most complicated, decorative, and practical knotted items to ease their boredom during long periods at sea. Many things, including rope ladders, bell pulls, and the much-admired hammocks, were traded at various ports for food, clothing, cigarettes, or alcohol.

The Feminist Movement

During the 1970's, the revival of the art of macramé coincided with the feminist movement, which reflected a broader cultural division in the pursuit of sexual and financial freedom while bucking traditional gender expectations of motherhood and marriage. Many of these women pushed the bar with their macramé creations to exhibit uninhibited, awe-inspiring creative crafts that were sometimes beyond imagination.

Macramé and Anti-Pollution

One such embellishment was the macramé owl's role in promoting the U.S. Forest Service's 1971 decision to stop pollution. Their slogan, "Give a hoot. Don't pollute!" is believed to have encouraged macramé crafters to create a variety of exciting and sometimes ridiculous representations of the Woodsy Owl mascot.

The New Age movement used macramé owls as Feng Shui symbols of good luck and wisdom that took the world by storm during the 1970's.

Modern-Day Macramé

In the 21st century, chic bohemianism has found a definitive connection to macramé, which is now closely linked to self-care and crafting with natural fibers. Social media, blogs, and e-commerce sites have played essential roles in reviving the modern art of macramé, which is fast becoming an exciting global knotting trend.

QUICK REFERENCE TABLE

For ease of reference, the table below clearly defines the three yarn crafts discussed above.

Hand yarn craft type	Definition
Crochet	Making yarn into a decorative fabric using a hooked needle.
Knitting	The art of forming fabric by looping yarn over two or more knitting needles.
Macramé	The skill of knotting cords or strings in patterns to create decorative objects.

EXCITING FACTS ABOUT CROCHET

- French woman Anne Vanier-Drüssel made the longest crochet chain, measuring 130 km (80.78 miles).
- American Lisa Gentry is recorded as the fastest crochet crafter, making 5,113 stitches in 30 minutes.
- Unlike many machine-yarn-produced products, crochet remains a hand-crafted skill.
- The most enormous crochet blanket in the world, measuring 12,195.511 square feet (3,133 square meters), was made in South Africa in 2015 to celebrate Mandela day.

THE KEY TAKEAWAY

Although the original birthplace of crochet is challenging to pinpoint, the yarn craft has gathered numerous followers through the ages to become one of the most popular and versatile hobbies of all time. Join me as we examine the unique and perhaps unexpected benefits of crochet.

2

BENEFITS OF CROCHET

Why crochet when you can buy ready-made items immediately without the fuss of making them?

Crocheting is an art in its own right. The yarn craft has been passed down for centuries from one family member to another, and many crafters still enjoy the creative versatility of crochet.

CRAFT AND SUPPORT

Crocheting is not only a great hobby, it also offers many benefits to your physical and mental health and well-being. Here are just some of the fantastic advantages crochet is believed to offer its crafters.

Helps Patients With Disabilities

The yarn art of crochet is just one of the many art types used by occupational therapists to treat patients with disabilities, injuries, and illnesses through the therapeutic use of frequent, repetitive activities. The daily tasks given to these patients reportedly help them recover their fine motor skills, improve their memory, and develop a sense of usefulness through growing their creative talents.

Reduces Anxiety and Stress

Almost everyone experiences stress and anxiety in their lives. However, when you do an activity you enjoy, such as crochet, your mind switches to its happy state and you begin to feel better about yourself. In addition, your heart rate and blood pressure are likely to drop as you participate in the rhythmic hand movements associated with crochet. Sitting quietly with your favorite beverage and a crochet project taking shape as you work, has been reported to release dopamine, the feel-good hormone responsible for relaxation and happiness. There's little that can compete with this sense of peace.

Ameliorates Depression

Many people suffering from depression could likely benefit from the positive upswing of crochet. When you are busy with any craft, including knitting and crochet, you become absorbed in following the pattern and watching the crafted object grow beneath your fingers. You get a sense of personal achievement that helps lift your spirits and brings a "ray of sunshine" into your life.

Encourages Mindfulness

The repetitive nature of crochet helps crafters to be mindful of the present as they follow patterns, count stitches, and keep track of their beautiful artwork. Without consciously meditating, you reap the benefits of having a peaceful mindset through the art of crocheting. Thus, crocheting forces you to stay focused and helps maintain the present status quo in which there is no time to look back to the past or ahead to the future. Instead, there is simply the now!

Slows Dementia

Crochet may slow the onset of dementia. Seniors specifically are likely to benefit from taking up knitting or crochet to help them maintain their mental faculties. What's more, crochet crafters can work independently at their individual pace and witness the tangible outcome of their efforts.

Repetitive crochet techniques and hand movements are believed to significantly help slow memory loss, prevent cognitive decline, and improve rational thought and mental reasoning.

Reduces Restlessness and Irritability

Crochet may be a positive, therapeutic outlet for irritation, boredom, and anger. In addition, the sense of peace and harmony elicited by crochet helps to reduce restlessness. Added to this is positive proof of your crafty efforts as you see your crocheted article take shape.

Builds Self-Esteem

We all want to feel useful, accepted, and productive. And by working up a unique crochet project, we can quickly achieve these goals.

Most people enjoy the feeling of accomplishment when they complete a specific task. You'll find pleasure and satisfaction when you make attractive, functional crochet projects, however simple these may be.

Crochet allows you to experiment with your unique color, style, and design choices—a great way to increase your productivity and sense of worth. There is little to beat the feeling of accomplishment you get when you complete a beautiful hand-crafted object that other people often admire.

Increases Productivity

Crochet has the fantastic effect of encouraging you to want to make more items. Each time you complete a crochet project, another is waiting to be made. You are likely to find crochet crafting addictive, to say the least.

Eases Insomnia

Crochet is a great way to spend those wakeful hours, especially since there's nothing worse than lying awake with nothing to occupy your mind and hands. Many insomniacs may benefit from the repetitive, rhythmic crochet movements, which are likely to calm the nerves and increase relaxation, thus improving sleep habits.

Builds Community Spirit

Many crochet crafters find a unique connection with like-minded crafters who share their ideas and crocheting pursuits. Sharing time with other crafters has the added benefit of growing new ideas and developing a solid support structure for all your craft adventures.

And for anyone seeking therapy benefits in a group setting, crochet is an ideal way to find people of a similar mindset. The yarn craft can also be a positive ice-breaker when meeting people for the first time.

Helps Process Grief

Keeping your hands and mind occupied during grief will likely offer you the added support you need to process your loss creatively, mindfully, and positively.

Offers Challenges

Taking on a new and exciting crochet challenge can benefit your psyche. A sense of venturing into unchartered waters will leave you wanting to discover more about the patterns you have chosen to work.

Encourages Creativity

Crochet encourages crafters to develop their unique patterning and design skills. Stitch versatility allows the crafter to make various beautiful objects without learning to read intricate patterns.

Helps Overcome Addictions

Learning to crochet can include support for overcoming specific addictions, like smoking. Keeping your hands and mind busy with your exciting new yarn craft venture means there's no time to light up a cigarette!

Promotes an Inexpensive Portable Craft

Crochet is a relatively low-cost, easy-to-learn craft you can do almost anywhere at any time.

What's more, this yarn craft is a beautiful way of making inexpensive, unique homemade gifts.

Appeals to all Ages

Crochet projects can be as simple or complex as you need. The craft is open to all age groups. Even young children can do finger-crochet, producing worthy efforts to make simple mats or scarves.

Surpasses Time

Crochet is a versatile craft that grows and changes throughout time to accommodate new ideas, colors, and styles. You will never be bored if you take up a worthwhile, exciting yarn craft like crochet.

Encourages a Lucrative Side Hustle

You may not know it, but you can sell your unique crochet projects at flea markets or on websites like Etsy. Dozens of Facebook groups will also allow you to sell and buy handmade items. Thus, most crafts, and especially crochet, have the potential to develop into a lucrative means of earning a steady income.

COMPARING CROCHET TO OTHER CRAFTS

There are many different crafts and hobbies available. However, some of these have more significant benefits than others. The best way to choose your preferred handcraft is by deciding on the type of things you want to make.

Choose knitting if you mainly want to make clothes for adults, babies, or children. Crochet, on the other hand, is quicker, easier, and ideal for making blankets, home wares, toys, or lacework.

You will find exciting patterns, from simple to more intricate and demanding styles. There are many stunning items to crochet, from hats, scarves, and fingerless mittens to cushion covers. You may also choose to make a stylish phone, laptop, or iPad cover. And why not try your hand at crocheting baby booties and small blankets?

Handcraft	Pros	Cons
Crochet	• Portable • Minimal tools—hooks and yarn • Quick and easy to complete most projects • Plenty of patterns available • Great for smaller items—scarves, socks, and hats • Successful for throws, rugs, shawls, and lacy doilies • Great for small Amigurumi toys • Mistakes are easier to fix • Improvisation works well with crochet • You can have more than one project on the go • Crochet articles don't stretch • Crochet yarn can be recycled and reused	• Can use more yarn than knitting in some projects • A firmer surface makes crochet less suitable for sweaters and certain types of clothing • You need to pay closer attention as you work a pattern • Crochet involves lots of stitch counting • The same stitches have different names in the US compared to the UK
Knitting	• Portable • Minimal tools—yarn, needles • Makes a more delicate fabric • Doesn't always need your full attention as you work • Mainly used for clothing—gloves, sweaters, and baby clothes • Knitted fabric, drapes well • Great for fitted garments • Knitting yarn can be reused	• Moderately expensive • Adequate yarn supplies need to be bought to make sure you don't run short • Harder to learn the craft • Challenging for left-handed crafters • Projects take a longer time to complete • Requires the use of both hands • Requires you to learn two basic stitches—knitting and purl • Lots of stitches on the needle at one time • Easier to drop stitches • Mistakes are harder to fix • Takes up space • Knitted projects stretch

Macramé	• Versatile • Liberating • Multipurpose—home and personal items • Great for decorative items • Used for gift-making • Therapeutic • Enhances mental abilities	• Expensive material • Selection of the material may be challenging • Difficult knotting techniques • Hard on the hands • The finished product is difficult to clean • Cord color can fade and fray • Cords can't be reused

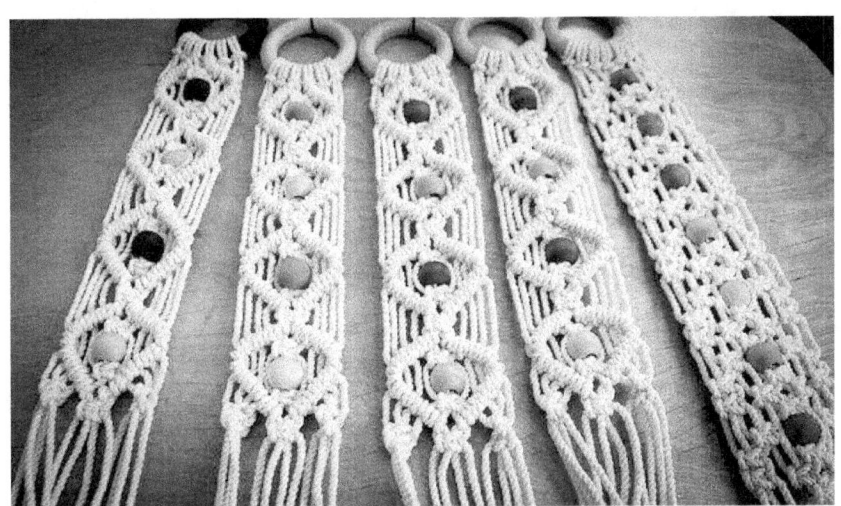

BUSINESS OPPORTUNITIES

Many crafters, including those who enjoy crochet, may wonder at some point whether their crafty, unique, hand-made creations are worth selling. As I am sure you will agree, extra income is always welcome if you are raising a family. But how do you find your target market, and where should you go to advertise and sell your creative goods?

Here are four of the most popular platforms to get your unique crochet and other crafty articles sold.

Platform 1: Friends and Family

Perhaps the most common place to start selling your creative work is to your family and friends, who understand the importance of your sideline business. They are more likely to support your efforts and buy some of your unique creations.

+ Positive Aspects

Having an enthusiastic, supportive family and friend base can make for an encouraging start to your business venture.

− Negative Aspects

No matter how positive your support base, there are a limited number of items your family and friends can buy. So it is unlikely that you will be able to sustain your business with such a narrow customer base.

The last thing you want is for awkwardness to seep into your close relationships if your family and friends begin to feel you are loading the responsibility for the success of your business onto their shoulders. You can't rely on family members and friends alone to help you keep your business up and running.

Platform 2: Craft Fairs and Flea Markets

Many crafters have very mixed reactions to craft fairs and markets—some boast of making a comfortable living with them, while others have experienced only disappointing results.

To sell in any market, you need an inventory of exciting products that will likely attract attention.

In addition, the price of your items should consider the labor intensity of the crochet article and the time and activities required to market it.

+ Positive Aspects

Most sales-minded people love interacting with potential customers at social events such as markets and fairs.

− Negative Aspects

You may need to do a lot of time-consuming research to find the best craft market for your crochet items. There is also a table or booth fee at every market or fair to consider. Thus, the goods you sell should cover the cost of making the items, including a percentage to cover the table or booth fee. It can be very disappointing, not to mention costly, if you end up with a loss instead of a profit.

Platform 3: Facebook

With the incredible power of social media, local buy-sell and exchange groups have made their debut on Facebook, which has its own marketplace too.

✛ Positive Aspects

Selling on your local Facebook group can be a quick and easy way to earn extra cash. When you sell made-to-order items, you are assured that stock will move quickly. And, in the event of no interest in your items, you have not lost any money.

━ Negative Aspects

Sadly, selling online doesn't mean customers won't disappoint you. You need to be assured of payment for the sale of your goods. Thus, you will need to put safeguards in place before exchanging goods for cash online. Always secure received orders with cash payment upfront.

Platform 4: E-Commerce Sites

Handcrafts, including crochet, have experienced a resurgence of interest in recent years, bringing specific selling sites such as Etsy to many crafters' attention. The beauty of the Etsy platform is that all items for potential sale reach a global market.

✛ Positive Aspects

Most of the shoppers on Etsy know what they are looking for and will usually pay accordingly.

These customers are also aware of the effort to make handcrafted goods. Thus, customers on these sites are prepared to order specific items on a made-to-order basis.

— Negative Aspects

The secret to success on the Etsy site is ensuring your products are beautifully photographed and described in detail. What's more, you must be sure you can meet any orders.

It's worth the effort to research the best options for making your products appeal to customers. However, like many other e-commerce platforms, operational changes and costs always exist.

An Etsy online shop is relatively easy to set up, so you don't need to build up an inventory. If you feel this idea is your best option, then get started. And, remember, don't waste time and energy on customers who try to bargain you down. If they don't want your unique item and don't appreciate its worth, pass them up immediately.

IS LEARNING TO CROCHET WORTH THE EFFORT?

The exciting thing about crochet is that besides being a stress-busting hobby, only one stitch needs to be learned to do your first project. In addition, costs are low, and you have dozens of free patterns from which to choose. Soon you will be making useful, attractive items for friends and family or keeping them as heirlooms.

To start, you can pick up inexpensive yarn from yard sales and thrift stores, which is ideal for learning and creating your first crochet projects. Then, in no time, you find yourself hooked on the exciting and highly versatile skills of crochet.

THE KEY TAKEAWAY

There are tons of positive aspects of learning to crochet. Crochet is considered one of the most preferred hobbies for its extensive health benefits, stress-busting, and confidence-boosting abilities. And, because the craft skill is easy to learn, you can produce some fantastic crochet objects relatively quickly. So, let's choose the correct pattern for your needs and interests.

CHOOSE YOUR FAVORITE PROJECT/PATTERN

R eading and understanding crochet patterns will boost your yarn craft skills to a new level. However, many crochet crafters will attest to having wasted time and money looking for the perfect pattern only to find it missing essential instructions or poorly written. To avoid these costly mishaps, shared here are some top tips for deciphering these challenging patterns that, at first glance, appear impossible to understand.

TIPS FOR YOUR BEST CHOICE OF PATTERN

You will find various helpful training videos. However, copying the examples does not allow you to learn to read the patterns. Once you understand crochet terminology and hieroglyphics, you will find any design easy to understand without a demonstration.

Note Stitches and Abbreviations

Most crochet pattern designers include a list of stitches and abbreviations, which act as your secret code for interpreting the pattern instructions. Before starting a crochet project, research any stitches with which you are unfamiliar. And you may find working up a small sampler will help you learn the stitches you will need for your project.

Pay attention to the designer's notes, giving tips for making the pattern work. For example, among other essential details for pattern success, you will find important information on whether the turning chains count as the first stitch of each new row.

Ask the Designer

You will likely find most crochet pattern designers willing to share their guidance and support to help you make a success of your chosen crochet project.

Make notes as you read through the pattern to confirm you remember the essential details once you start the project.

Facebook Crochet Groups

Connect with the crochet groups on Facebook. You may be pleasantly surprised to discover that an abundance of crochet and craft groups are only too willing to share their knowledge and expertise. So, if you don't ask, you won't know!

Your support group will also give you a heads-up when patterns are copyrighted. Remember never to share the entire pattern on a public website to avoid copyright infringement.

Divide the Pattern Into Segments

Sometimes, dividing the pattern into manageable sections may help with reading and understanding the instructions more easily. For example, if your crochet pattern reads as follows.

Ch 3, dc into the next st, ch 3, skip next sc, *(2sc, ch 3, dc) in the next ch space, repeat from * to the second last ch space. (2sc, ch 3, dc) in the last ch space. Turn.

You may find it works better to mark specific areas of the pattern to make it easier to understand and read. What's more, the crochet pattern now appears less overwhelming. In this way, you are less likely to miss essential pattern steps.

Ch 3, /dc into the next st, /ch 3, skip next sc, /*(2sc, ch 3, dc) in the next ch space, / repeat from * to the second last ch space./ (2sc, ch 3, dc) in the last ch space. /Turn.

Write Down the Pattern

Another suggestion is to write each pattern step into a little notebook and cross each step out as you finish it.

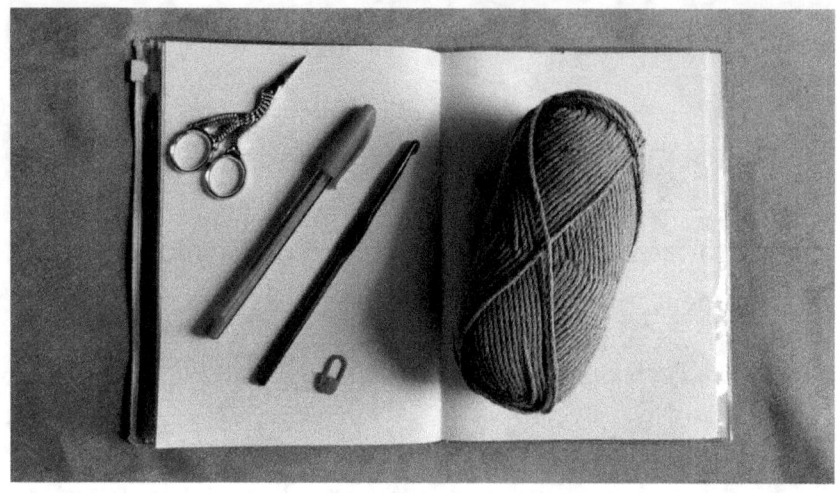

PARENTHESES, REPEATS, AND BRACKETS

Let's break down the meaning of these well-used crochet symbols.

Parentheses ( ) instruct you to follow the instructions inside the parenthesis in the same stitch. E.g., (Sc, 3dc) into the next stitch.

Repeats are marked with asterisks *, which signal where you start the repetition after the asterisk. E.g., *Sc in next ch 1, skip one and repeat from * across the row.

Sometimes, asterisks indicate you repeat the instruction after the first asterisk until the beginning of the last double asterisk. E.g., Sc 2 *(skip 1, dc 3)** to the last 2 st, sc 2.

Brackets [] recommend you do the instruction inside the brackets several times. E.g., [sk next st, 2sc into next dc] 4 times.

Once you have broken up the pattern, try to visualize the stitches before you make them. This idea will not only help you quickly notice any errors but will help you walk through each step. E.g., two dc in the next st means you will make two double crochet in the next stitch.

IMPORTANT CROCHET TERMS

Some crochet designers use their own unique abbreviations, so be sure to double-check the pattern before starting a project. Then, note any unusual abbreviations and look for information on any new terms.

You will often find a list of crochet abbreviations at the beginning and end of the pattern.

Term	Description
*	Replicate the instructions after the asterisk, as instructed.
**	Duplicate the commands in the middle of the asterisks as often as needed.
{ }	Work directions between the brackets as required.
[ ]	Work instructions in the brackets as instructed.
( )	Work instructions within the parentheses as ordered or work a stitch group into the next space or stitch, as required.

US/UK ABBREVIATIONS AND TERMS

Crochet terms differ from country to country, which can make pattern-reading quite challenging. British and Australian designers usually use UK terms, while US and Canadian crochet patterns are written in US terms.

Although both terminologies use similar terms, they often mean very different things. The main difference between US and UK crochet terms is the starting point.

- US terms start with single crochet, which in UK terminology refers to double crochet. Thus UK crochet terms are one step up from their US counterparts.
- Another difference is that the US terms refer to the number of yarnovers drawing up a loop. However, UK terms refer to the number of loops on the hook.
- The only terms standard in both terminologies are the chain (ch) and the slip stitch (ss/sl st).

Figuring out if a crochet pattern is written in US or UK terms can be a little daunting. However, here are several valuable tips to help beginner crochet crafters decide a pattern's country of origin.

- If single crochet (sc) stitches are used, the pattern uses US terms.

- When a pattern uses half treble stitches, it's written in UK terms.
- Patterns using "gauge" and "skip a stitch" are written in US terminology. UK patterns refer to "tension" and "miss a stitch."
- Where patterns, diagrams, and graphs are included, always check that the terminology in the written pattern matches what the graphic symbols show.

Many vintage patterns use UK terminology.

Crochet crafters worldwide should know the difference between acronyms and terms commonly used in the US, Canada, and the UK.

Understanding these terms and abbreviations will ensure that you can adjust your pattern or design accordingly.

US/Canada	UK
slip stitch (sl st)	slip stitch (ss)
single crochet (sc)	double crochet (dc)
half double crochet (hdc)	half treble crochet (htr)
double crochet (dc)	treble crochet (tr)
treble crochet (tr)	double treble crochet (dtr)
double treble crochet (dtr)	treble treble crochet (trtr)
US	UK/Canada
gauge	tension
yarn over (yo)	yarn over hook (yoh)

PRACTICE DILIGENTLY

You have possibly heard the phrase "Practice makes perfect." To a large extent, it is true. The more you practice, the better you become at reading the crochet patterns, and the more fluid and skillful your movements are.

It's a good idea to do a trial run with an extra length of yarn so that you can master the stitches before you start the actual project. And though this activity may seem a waste of time, it will save you hours of frustration in the long run.

Crochet instructions are sometimes written in the text without abbreviations. These instructions can also appear in a graph or chart format using specific crochet symbols. Reading any crochet pattern, regardless of the form, allows you to work on almost any crochet project and improve your confidence and skill.

CROCHET SYMBOL CHART

The crochet symbol chart visually depicts the crochet pattern. Each row or round is displayed, stitch by stitch, using a specific symbol to show each stitch. Once you understand the meaning of the strange-looking symbols, you will find it easy to read the pattern and follow the instructions.

So, single crochet may be depicted by "sc", "x", or "+".

 # Crochet Symbols

⊖ = chain (ch)

• = slip stitch (sl st)

X or + = single crochet (sc)*

T = half double crochet (hdc)

Ŧ = double crochet (dc)

Ŧ = treble crochet (tr)

Ŧ = double treble crochet (dtr)

⋏ = sc2tog

⋔ = sc3tog

⋀ = dc2tog

⋔ = dc3tog

() = 3-dc cluster

() = 3-hdc cluster/puff st/bobble

() = 5-dc popcorn

= 5-dc shell

() = ch-3 picot

= front post dc (FPdc)

= back post dc (BPdc)

⌢ = worked in back loop only**

⌣ = worked in front loop only**

There are several ways to learn to crochet. Many people, including crafters, are visual learners who find image-based rather than text-based instructions easier to understand. So, if you are a visual learner, the crochet chart may work well for you.

Crochet patterns often include both symbols and written instructions. Thus, although you may find text directions easier to understand, it can be helpful to have visual symbols and charts to help you understand the crochet instructions. In any event, extra information, in the form of a chart that supplements written instructions, is handy to have.

The exciting news is that once you can interpret the crochet symbol chart, you are all set to use any crochet pattern. The great thing about symbolic diagrams is that they are not language-based. So, despite language differences, crochet symbol charts open up many crafty opportunities as the books share common crochet symbols.

A SPECIAL NOTE TO OUR LEFT-HANDED CROCHET CRAFTERS

Adapting patterns for left-handed crafters need not be as challenging as you think.

Most crochet symbol charts are written for right-handed crafters. Left-handed crochet crafters must reverse the pattern.

You may want to make a physically switched design reproduction. Here are some valuable tips to help you flip your design.

You should follow simple, symmetric crochet patterns as they are written but reverse the direction in which you work. More intricate designs will need to be changed in their entirety.

In addition, left-handed crafters must remember to switch all patterns detailing words to correct the letters. So, when the pattern instructs you to work from right to left, left-handed crochet crafters should work in the opposite direction from left to right.

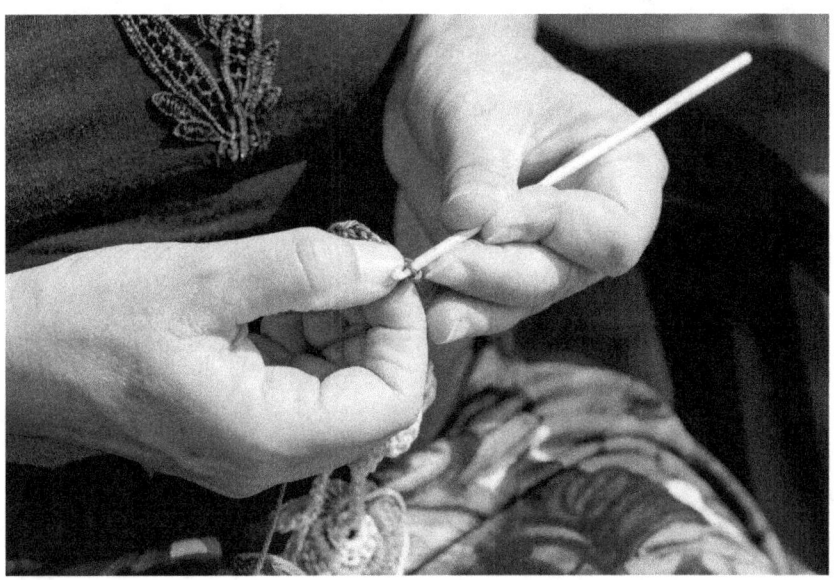

Symbol charts are worked in the opposite direction to the printed or graphic instructions. In effect, you make a mirror image of the pattern. So, how do left-handed crafters reverse a pattern? Some crafters can switch the designs in their minds as they remind themselves to work in the opposite direction. However, not all left-handed crochet crafters can do this, and that's okay. What you will do is create a mirror image of the pattern.

Left-handed crafters can use photo editing tools on their computers to flip images or reverse videos using the "horizontal flip" button. If you don't have photo editing tools on your computer, try using a glass window. First, print the image you want to use. Tape the picture to a window. Then, trace the image onto the back of the sheet.

Remember to reverse any letters to make sure they read correctly on the reverse side of the pattern.

As for written patterns, left-handed crafters may highlight specific clues indicating the work direction. For example, "join yarn in the right corner" should be reversed to read "join yarn in the left corner". And "work into the wrong side of your work" should read "work into the right side of your work".

CROCHET ABBREVIATIONS

Crochet patterns are designed to create specific objects and are often written in crochet shorthand terms. These standardized abbreviations make it easier for the crafter to follow the instructions. If you find shorthand terms challenging to identify, take a quick look at the terms included here for your convenience. As you continue to use the abbreviations, you'll likely find that you memorize many of these crochet craft acronyms.

CROCHET ABBREVIATION CHART

Abbreviation	Description	Abbreviation	Description
alt	alternate	inc	increase
approx	approximately	lp	loop
beg	begin/beginning	m	marker
bet	between	MC	main color
BL/BLO	back loop/back loop only	pat/patt	pattern
bob	bobble	prev	previous
BP	back post	rem	remaining
CC	contrast color	rep	repeat
ch	chain	rnd	round
ch-sp	chain space	RS	right side
CL	cluster	sc	single crochet

cont	continue	sc2tog	single crochet two stitches together
dc	double crochet	tbl	through the back of the loop
dc2tog	double crochet two stitches together	tch/t-ch	turning chain
FL/FLO	front loop/front loop only	tog	together
foll	following	trb	treble
FP	front post	trb2tog	treble crochet two stitches together
hdc	half double crochet	WS	wrong side
hdc2tog	half double crochet two stitches together	yo/yoh	yarn over/yarn over hook

TUNISIAN CROCHET

The unique technique of Tunisian or Afghan crochet may lead you to believe its origins are in northern Africa. However, this crochet subset is considered to have started in France, where, during the 1800s, publications showed Tunisian stitches. Later in the same century, Tunisian crochet was carried out in England and Western Europe.

- The Tunisian crochet technique is a mix of knitting and crochet using a longer hook than in traditional crochet.

- This type of crochet is often used for more extensive articles such as afghans, throws, and floor coverings.
- The craft usually works with many stitches on the hook.
- Each row is worked twice and counted as one row. The required number of stitches are first looped onto the hook; then, each stitch is worked off the hook until the row is complete.
- Pull firmly on the yarn to make sure the edges are neat.
- Work double crochet across the final row in your project to give a professional finish.
- A border is sometimes added to the finished article to stop the edges from curling.

Here is a schedule of the important abbreviations used in most Tunisian patterns and designs.

Tunisian Crochet Abbreviations

Abbreviation	Description
etss	extended Tunisian simple stitch
FwP	forward pass
RetP	return pass
tdc	Tunisian double crochet
tfs	Tunisian full stitch
thdc	Tunisian half double crochet
tks	Tunisian knit stitch
tps	Tunisian purl stitch
trs	Tunisian reverse stitch
tsc	Tunisian single crochet
tss	Tunisian simple stitch
tslst	Tunisian slip stitch
ttr	Tunisian treble crochet
ttw	Tunisian twisted

COMMON MEASUREMENTS

As with all crafts, keeping a close watch on the size of the crochet article is vital for the success of the finished product.

Measurement	Description
"/in	inch/inches
cm	centimeter
g	gram
m	meter
mm	millimeter
oz	ounce
yd	yard

OTHER EXCITING CROCHET OPTIONS

If you have been bitten by the "crochet bug" and want to extend your skills, you might be surprised to know that there are several different crochet techniques. So, to further pique your interest, here are just a few varieties you might want to try.

Colorwork Techniques

Your love of color, design, and pattern can soar to great heights as you extend your crochet skills even further.

Technique	Description
Fair Isle Crochet	Originally a knitting technique, Fair Isle has become a much-admired and richly detailed crochet style for afghans and attractive winter woolies.
Overlay Crochet	This technique combines rich colors and textures to create the unique stained glass effect commonly used in mandalas.
Reversible Crochet	A neat, colorful pattern is created by crocheting two separate pieces of fabric and joining these to create a new and exciting design.
Tapestry Crochet	The technique is worked with a base color layered with many colors to create fascinating patterns and designs. Tapestry crochet creates sturdy items that are perfect for sculptural creations.

Lace Crochet Techniques

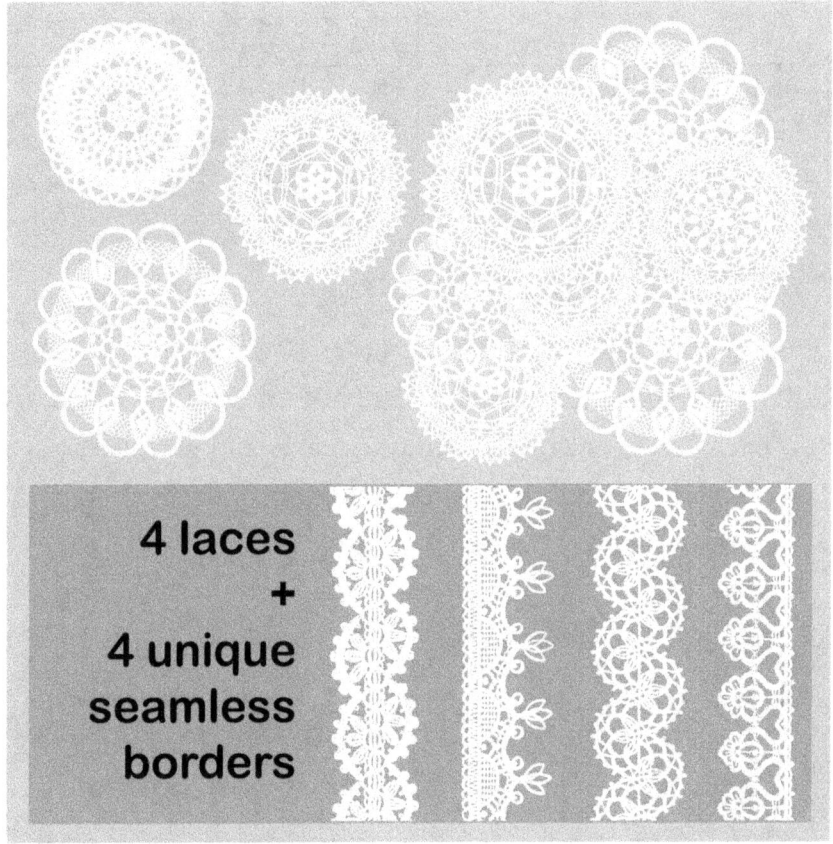

Lace crochet often comes in various attractive designs with clever placement of holes on the surface of the item. Traditionally, these techniques used fine cotton and small hooks, but you can design and create anything using your imagination and unique crocheting style.

Technique	Description
Filet Crochet	Creative techniques use double crochet and space to create gorgeous lace designs perfect for attractive coasters, comfy baby blankets, and unique garments.
Irish Lace Crochet	Vintage techniques add a touch of nostalgia and old-world glamour to beautiful curtains, tablecloths, and various other delicate items.

Other Techniques

Not surprisingly, crochet techniques have developed many different forms to encompass plenty of interesting designs to suit every crochet crafter's unique needs and creative skills. Here is a delightful example of an exquisitely formed, tiny Amigurumi rabbit.

Technique	Description
Amigurumi	The Japanese art of making tiny toys, ornaments, and a variety of bowls and other fascinating items is another popular crochet technique.
Bavarian Crochet	This technique is suitable for high-texture, beautiful and colorful designs for gorgeous blankets and one-of-a-kind quality items such as jackets and shawls.
Freeform Crochet	A modern and utterly patternless technique, free-form crochet is just what it says. Any combination of styles, colors, designs, and yarns can be used to create unique items.

The attractive Bavarian headband with its charming embellishment makes an appealing fashion statement.

Crochet craft extends to free-form creative designs in the most unexpected places.

THE KEY TAKEAWAY

As you can see, there are various stunning and functional crochet projects from which to choose. Now that you are hooked on crochet and have a good idea about patterns, designs, and crocheting styles, you are ready to start putting your crochet tools together.

4

YOUR TOOL DRAWER

Once you have learned to relax and enjoy the satisfyingly creative crochet craft, you will want to familiarize yourself with the basic tools essential for the success of your first project. Various crochet hook designs are available. These may be obtained from your local craft shop or purchased online. Unfortunately, not all hooks are equal, and you may find the choice quite disconcerting. So, here are several tips to help you make the best selection for your perfect project.

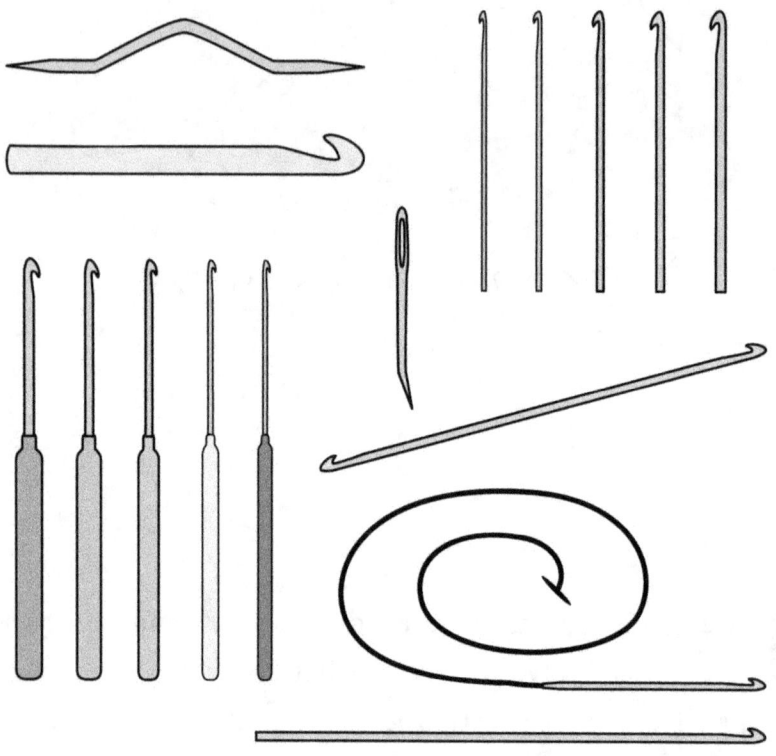

ESSENTIAL MATERIALS

You should invest in a basic crochet tool kit to crochet projects without stress. For starters, you need crochet hooks, a hook organizer, a pair of scissors, stitch markers, a yarn needle, and suitable yarn.

CROCHET

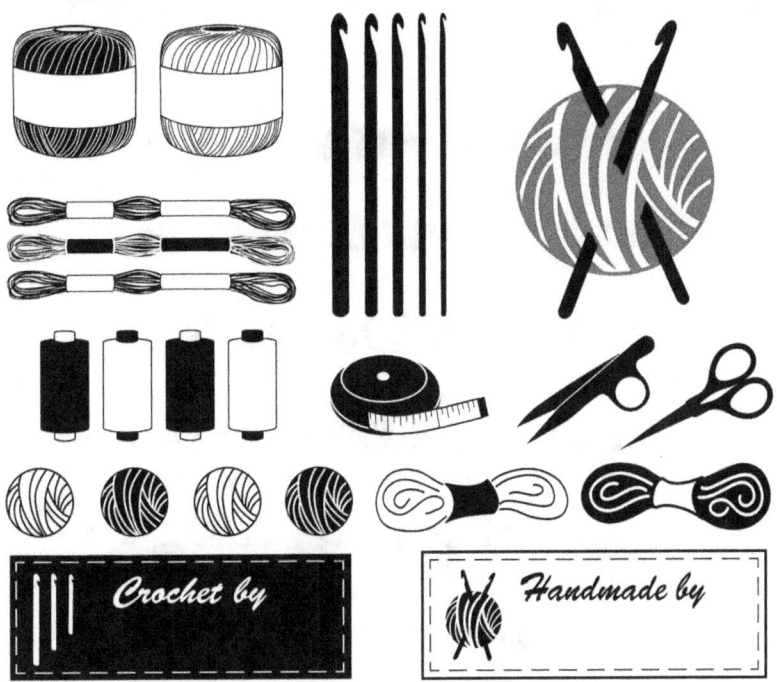

Crochet Hooks

There are three essential aspects to consider when choosing a crochet hook.

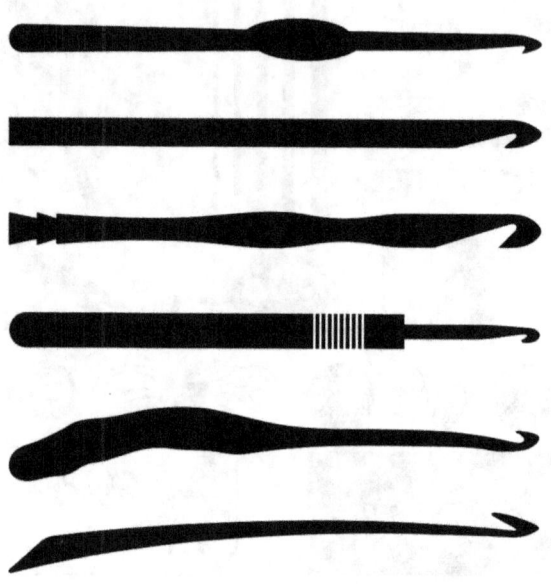

▷ Size

Depending on your crochet project and the yarn weight you use, you should select a suitable hook for the task. The larger the crochet hook, the bigger the stitches will be. Fortunately, the choice isn't too difficult as most yarns and patterns suggest specific-sized hooks.

The following hook conversion chart is an easy reference, especially for beginner crochet crafters.

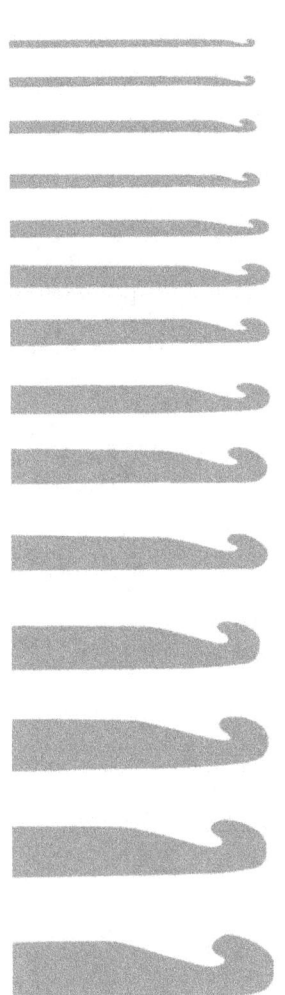

Crochet Hook Conversion Chart		
Metric	**USA**	**UK**
2.00 mm	-	14
2.25 mm	1 / B	13
2.50 mm	-	12
2.75 mm	C	11
3.00 mm	-	11
3.25 mm	D	10
3.50 mm	4 / E	9
3.75 mm	F	-
4.00 mm	6	8
4.25 mm	G	-
4.50 mm	7	7
5.00 mm	8 / H	6
5.50 mm	9 / I	5
6.00 mm	10 / J	4
6.50 mm	10 1/2 / K	3
7.00 mm	-	2
8.00 mm	-	0
9.00 mm	15 / N	00
10.00 mm	P	000
15.75 mm or 16mm	Q	-

▷ Hook Type

Crochet hooks come in two distinctive shapes. Inline hooks have pointed heads, and the shaft and handle are in a straight line. Tapered hooks have a rounded head that may make crocheting easier.

▷ Material

Crochet hooks are made from various materials. There is no single, suitable material, but the choice of material changes how the hook feels in your hand.

Let's take an in-depth look at the hook options. You will find crochet needles or hooks made from various materials, including plastic, wood, metal, and glass. Most standard crochet hooks are about six inches long.

Hook Type	Description
Aluminum	The most popular inexpensive hooks are made from anodized aluminum and come in various attractive colors. These hooks will likely last a lifetime. Versatile and affordable, these crochet hooks are perfect for beginners. In addition, a wide range of hook sizes makes these hooks suitable for almost any crochet project.
Plastic	All-plastic hooks are trendy because they are readily available and relatively inexpensive. In addition, some hooks have small lights to give you better visibility in low-light conditions. These hooks range in size from B to S (2.25 to 20 mm).
Steel	These hooks start at the most petite sizes and are perfect for working with fine yarn, cotton, and silk. The hooks are often used to crochet dainty, attractive doilies and delicate lacy curtains.
Tunisian	This crochet type is a combination of knitting and crocheting that uses many stitches on the hook. Therefore, these hooks are longer than usual, and some have long cables attached. Tunisian hooks come in different thicknesses and lengths, depending on the specific project for which they will be used.
Wood	Wooden hooks are gorgeous, and these may be the best choice if you prefer to use natural materials. Hooks made of rosewood or birch can last a long time. Hooks made of pine, maple, or bamboo are suitable alternatives.
Ergonomic Hook	Combination hooks with a metal head and a plastic or rubber handle are more ergonomic. In addition, many of these hooks are more comfortable to handle and easier to use for extended periods.

THE BEST ERGONOMIC CROCHET HOOKS

If you suffer from carpal tunnel or have hand and wrist challenges, you may find one of the following ergonomic hooks ideal to continue with your favorite crochet projects without undue pain and discomfort.

Ergonomic hook	Description	Pros	Cons
Clover Amour	• Comfortable handle that fits snugly in your hand. • Lightweight, smooth aluminum that doesn't snag yarn. • An array of attractive colors identifies each hook size for easy recognition.	• A smooth shaft that offers less resistance. • Ergonomic handle allows for more extended periods of crafting. • Lightweight makes the hook more manageable to handle without straining your wrists.	• Raised letters on the handle may cause blisters when used with a knife-hold. • The large handle may not suit beginners.
Addi Swing	• Ideal ergonomic shape for a natural grip and more prolonged use. • The soft plastic handle is sturdy and flexible. • Different sizes are color-coded for more accessible identification. • Nickel-coated hook shaft glides easily through yarn.	• The ergonomic design takes the stress out of crocheting. • Hooks slip easily through yarn.	• Hooks can be heavy for some crafters. • The shorter shaft is not suitable for projects with many stitches on the hook.

Athena Elements	• Highly favored by crafters suffering from carpal tunnel. • High-grade thermoplastic rubber makes the handles more manageable and more comfortable to grip. • The longer shaft works easily for more stitches. • Useful for working with larger yarn. • Smooth finish that doesn't snag yarn.	• The full-length needle is well supported in the handle. • A sturdy, non-slip handle causes less tension in the wrist. • The longer shaft holds more stitches. • Great for Amigurumi projects that require tighter stitches. • Available in all popular sizes.	• Handle may feel sticky when first used. • Only come in the inline variety, so it may not suit crafters preferring tapered hooks.
Furl's	• A soft handle-grip helps alleviate hand and wrist pain while crocheting. • A longer hook facilitates an increased number of stitches. • Hooks glide easily through the yarn.	• Available in all sizes. • Sizes are color-coded for ease of reference. • Great for beginner crochet crafters. • Offers pain-free crocheting. • Easy to use.	• Easily rolls off the work surface if not secured. • The shallow head makes it difficult to keep thicker yarns on the hook.

Teamoy	• Suitable for crafters with arthritis or carpal tunnel. • Lightweight tool that causes no strain to your fingers and wrists while crocheting. • Soft rubber grip for added comfort. • Ideal for beginners and experienced crafters. • Smooth, professional finish to make sure no yarn snags. • Available in sizes from 2.0 mm to 6.0 mm.	• Color-coded sizes for easy recognition. • Sizes are marked on the hook handles. • Exchangeabl e rubber grip.	• Only nine sizes available.
Boye	• A great option for those with carpal tunnel. • The smooth rounded head doesn't split or snag yarn. • Color-coded handles. • Sizes US B (2.25 mm) to N (10 mm).	• Soft rubber grip. • Variety of hook sizes. • Color-coded handles. • Rounded head.	• The tapered hook may not suit crafters who prefer the inline variety.

Hook Organizer

It's a good idea to keep your crochet tools safe and easily accessible by placing them in a simple bag.

Scissors

When planning your crochet tool kit, scissors may not be one of the first things you consider. Dull scissors tend to fray yarn ends. Consider the blade length. For yarn craft, the best scissors should have a short blade, an easy grip, and be easy to store. Therefore, choose a small pair of sharp scissors that cut cleanly. You may find stork scissors the best choice.

Stitch Markers

The tiny plastic or interlocking metal clips help track increases, decreases, stitches, and rows. Stitch markers take the monotony out of continually counting stitches and rows.

Notebook and Pen

It's a great idea to keep notes of patterns and keep track of specific pattern details by jotting these down in a handy notebook.

YARN

Some kind of yarn is essential for any crochet project. But, how do you choose the suitable type for the job? There are plenty of different yarn types from which to choose. Fortunately, your pattern should give you a clear indication of which to use.

Your yarn choice depends on your specific project, style, color, and the final unique effect you would like to achieve. Inexpensive medium worsted weight acrylic yarn, available in an array of gorgeous shades, is ideal for most beginner crochet crafters.

Yarn is packaged in hanks, balls, or skeins. Hanks was coiled into large circles and twisted into a plait-like shape before being labeled. Yarn balls are formed by winding the yarn to create a globe shape. If you choose to crochet with yarn skeins, you will likely find a rainbow selection of threads in your local craft store. The yarn varieties will astonish you. Like many other crochet crafters, you will quickly become obsessed with the desire for various beautiful yarns in each of your magnificent craft projects. Here are some helpful yarn tips to get your crochet creativity into top form.

Yarn comes in a variety of sizes and shapes. Lace yarn is the lightest and most delicate, being cobwebby thin, while the thickest thread, jumbo, has the circumference of a soda can.

Natural Fibers

All-natural yarns are either animal or plant-sourced. Suitable yarns include those from merinos, alpacas, llamas, silk-worms, and sheep. You may want to choose an appropriate thread for your project from the list below.

▷ **Merino**

Among the more costly yarn types, Merino is a perfect choice for specific crochet projects. Merino yarn attributes include:

- **Softness**

Merino wool is three times softer than silk. The elastic fibers of high-quality Merino stay soft after every wash without needing a fabric softener.

- **Elastic**

The natural elasticity of Merino fabrics is due to their unique molecular structure, which allows for freedom of movement and improved comfort. Merino fabric can stretch by as much as 50% and then regain its original shape without damaging the fabric.

- **Absorbent**

Merino's highly developed moisture-wicking qualities ensure the fabric absorbs moisture in a humid environment and re-releases it in drier conditions. Therefore, Merino wool may be the perfect fabric for any weather and climate type.

- **Ideal Temperature Control**

Merino fabric has low heat conductivity. Thus, it feels as if it has a built-in temperature control. Tiny air pockets form in the material, which keeps the wearer warm in cold conditions and more comfortable when the weather is warmer.

Favored by Bedouins in the Sahara Desert, Merino fabric has several other uses besides clothing, including mattress-making.

- **Hypoallergenic**

Merino is the ideal fabric for asthma and allergy sufferers. Due to the fabric's ability to regulate temperature, it is also believed that wearing Merino in contact with the skin will help reduce eczema. In addition, skin itch and irritation are likely significantly reduced when wearing Merino fabric.

▷ Wool

Fiber obtained from sheep is warm and durable. The fabric usually softens with careful washing. However, wool fabrics require proper, safe handling to avoid fabric stretching. Pure wool is ideal for mittens, socks, sweaters, and scarves. It is also one of the most popular fibers for baby clothing, hats, and blankets.

▷ Alpaca

Alpacas are South American camelids that produce high-quality fleece with excellent benefits. The fiber obtained from alpaca coats is believed to be one of the coziest known natural fibers and makes perfect insulation against the cold. In addition, the soft, warm yarn from alpaca fleece is ideal for knitting and weaving.

▷ Angora

The exquisitely expensive soft fiber known as angora comes from rabbits of the same name. Although the yarn quality is magnificent, it has no stretch and can sometimes cause allergic reactions to wearers.

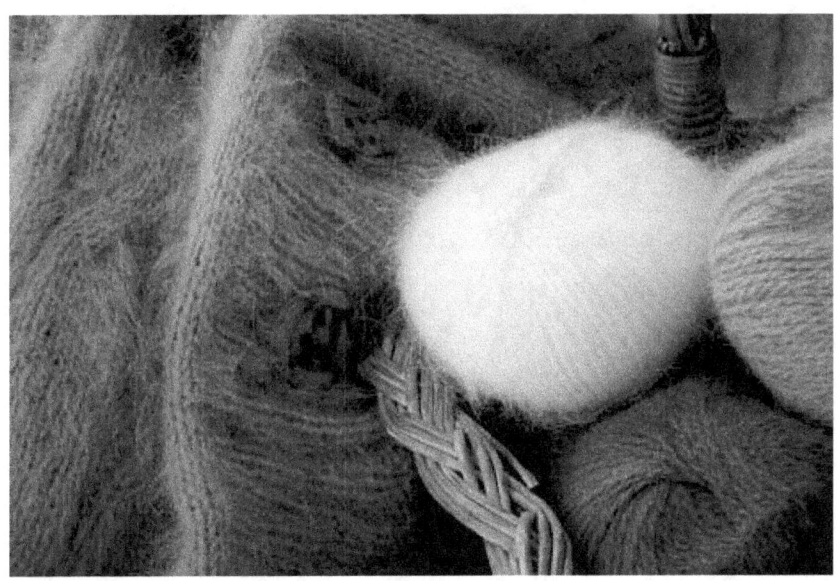

▷ Cashmere

Another highly favored craft yarn is cashmere obtained from goats. The fiber is suitable for garments close to the skin and is also ideal for baby blankets, hats, and jackets.

▷ Mohair

The expensive and popular natural fiber mohair comes from Angora goats. The fabric is durable and warm, making it ideal for many clothing items.

▷ Silk

This beautiful, trendy, and highly sought-after fabric is usually used for fine clothing and attractive bedding. Although seldom used for crochet because of its expense and delicate thread status, silk can be a stunning embellishment to jazz up special crochet projects.

▷ Cotton

The natural fiber cotton is plant-based. Cotton yarn is hard-wearing, durable, and washable. Crocheted items from cotton may include easy-wear items like socks and vests, among other things. You can also use cotton yarn for making attractive tablecloths. Fine cotton threads are ideal for dainty lace projects and doilies.

Manufactured Fibers

Some fibers are made from plastics or petroleum by-products. These include nylon, rayon, polyester, and acrylic. The artificial threads are longer-wearing and easy to care for, clean, and store.

▷ Acrylic

The most versatile yarn manufactured from chemicals, acrylic is durable and washable. Acrylic is considered the ideal yarn for beginner crocheters to make gloves, hats, sweaters, throws, and dozens of other valuable items.

▷ **Blended Fibers**

Several trendy manufactured yarns from acrylic and cotton blends have become popular for crochet projects.

The inexpensive yarn is an ideal yarn choice for gloves, hats, and small rugs.

YARN COLOR

Beginner crochet crafters should consider choosing lighter colors when they are starting out learning to crochet. Neutral yarn makes stitch and row count easier. Errors can also be quickly spotted and corrected.

Yarn Dye, Lot, and Yardage

Yarn prices vary according to the yarn type; thus, as a beginner, you should consider less expensive yarn choices for your first project. Cotton, wool, and acrylic yarns are not only less costly but also offer a wide array of magnificent color choices.

Each yarn type has a specific yardage per ball. Establish how many balls you need, ensuring each ball has similar yardage. Also, make sure you have enough yarn of the same dye lot for your pattern or project requirements. The dye lot is designated a specific number that is usually printed on the yarn label. Starting with smaller, more manageable projects will make sure you learn the essential crocheting skills quickly with minimal frustration and fuss.

Yarn Labels

Most yarn labels show fiber content and proper hook size for best results. The information is usually clearly displayed on the yarn label.

What's more, there are usually care instructions and the yarn ply, which is the number of strands twisted together to show the particular brand of yarn.

When using a crochet pattern, consider making a small sample to check the yarn gauge against that shown on the label. If the piece is too small, try using a larger hook.

Yarn Ethics

Understanding the yarn source will help you make an informed choice about whether it suits your personal crochet principles. Eco-friendly plant threads from bamboo or cotton make easy-to-use and suitable crochet yarn options.

Yarn Tension

When you first start crocheting, keeping an even yarn tension may be somewhat challenging. Allowing the yarn to move freely over the fingers of your yarn hand will maintain an even thread flow, which should neither be too loose nor too tight. However, as with all new ventures, practice makes perfect. Although important in most crochet projects, yarn tension is a personal preference. Each crochet crafter has a unique hook grip which plays a vital role in maintaining crochet fabric tension.

WORSTED WEIGHT YARN

The medium-weight worsted yarn is the most suitable for almost any crochet project. In addition, the yarn is regarded as an ideal all-purpose yarn that is perfect for sweaters, gloves, socks, hats, and scarves.

The Craft Yarn Council developed a standardized yarn weight system to make sure that all yarn meets the same degree of excellence. Thus, each yarn weight is assigned a specific number ranging from zero (thinnest) to seven (thickest). Many patterns refer to yarn numbers. For example, worsted weight yarn is assigned the number 4, making it the middle child in the yarn family, which gives about 16–20 stitches every 4 inches worked.

When shopping for yarn, look for the number 4 or the word "worsted" on the yarn label. If neither of these details is displayed, check if the gauge falls into the 16–20 stitches per 4 inches. Worsted yarns are sometimes also called Aran or Afghan.

The Importance of Plies

All yarn comprises a specific number of strands. So, lace has a single strand and is called one ply. The thicker the yarn, the more strands are twisted together, and the heavier the yarn weight. Thus, worsted weight yarn has four strands and is also called 4-ply.

Yarn Weights

Yarn weight is decided by yarn thickness, which dictates the most suitable hook size for your crochet project.

The yarn chart indicates the ideal hook size for each yarn type.

Yarn	Written	Hook Sizes	Us Sizes	Uk Sizes
LACE 0	0: Lace or Thread, Coweb, Lace, Light, Fingering/Fingering	Steel or regular hook: 1.4 – 2.25 mm	Steel or regular hook: 2 – 14 steel or B – 1 regular	Steel or regular hook: 1 ½ – 7 steel or 13 – 14 regular
SUPER FINE 1	1: Super Fine or Fingering, Sock, Baby	2.25 – 3.5 mm	B – 1 C – 2 D – 3 E – 4	Steel: 1 ½ Regular: 10 – 13
FINE 2	2: Fine or Sport, Baby	3.5 – 4.5 mm	E – 4 F – 5 G – 6 7	7 – 9
LIGHT 3	3: Light or DK (Double knit), Light Worsted	4.5 – 5.5 mm	7 H – 8 I – 9	5 – 7
MEDIUM 4	4: Medium or Worsted, Aran, Triple Knit (rare), Fisherman, Afgahn	5.5 – 6.5 mm	I – 9 J – 10 K – 10.5	3 – 5
BULKY 5	5: Bulky or Chunky, Craft, Rug, Double Double Knit (rare)	6.5 – 9 mm	K – 10.5 L – 11 M/N - 13	00 – 3
SUPER BULKY 6	6: Super Bulky or Roving	9 mm – 15 mm	M/N – 13 N/P – 15 O P/Q	00 or 000

THE KEY TAKEAWAY

Setting up for your crochet craft takes time and energy, but once you have the essential tools, you are on your way to crocheting success. Now, it's time to learn the standard crochet stitches that form the foundation for many patterns.

HOW TO START—BASICS

B y now, you are probably all set to make a start on your first crochet project. But, as with any new venture, the air of excitement and suspense will probably spur you on to grab a yarn ball and hook to get started without delay.

Using light-colored worsted weight yarn is best to make sure you can see the stitches as you work. But first, check the yarn label and hook size for compatibility with the specific project.

In addition to the essential tools for crochet craft discussed in Chapter Four, it's important to know you should hold the hook in a specific manner to work your best craft magic.

HOLDING THE HOOK

As with all crafts, each crochet crafter has a unique grip on their trade tool, directly influencing the crochet fabric's tension. Most crochet crafters fall into one of the two main hook-holding groups, whether left-handed or right-handed.

Don't despair if you have no idea how to grip a crochet hook. Instead, please pick up your crochet hook and see which way feels best to hold it as you work. Gripping the hook in the most comfortable way will help you to work with ease, speed, and comfort.

Right-Handed Crochet Crafters

Although there is no fixed rule for hook grip, here are two easy-to-follow hook-holding instructions.

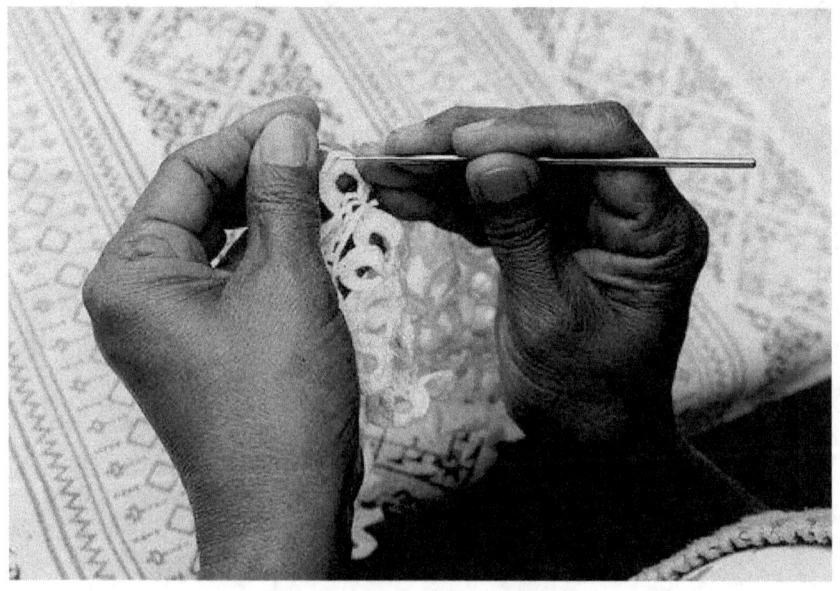

▷ Pencil Grip

If you grip your crochet hook as you would a pencil, you will likely find it easier to work your hook from above, the stitches pushing down as you perform each stitch.

If you are a right-handed crafter, you can grasp the hook in your right hand, between your index finger and thumb. Allow the crochet hook end to rest on your middle finger while your upper index finger supports the shaft and your other fingers remain below for added working support.

▷ Knife Grip

Alternatively, if you grip your hook in your right hand, the same way you would hold a knife, you will probably work into the front of your stitches.

Grip the hook in your right hand, with your dominant index finger resting on the hook's shaft near the hook end, while the shaft end rests below your index finger in the palm of your hand. The other fingers of the same hand firmly grip the hook and add working support.

Left-Handed Crochet Crafters

Left-handed crafters can follow a similar procedure above, using their left hand.

Many left-handed crafters have mastered crochet and are willing to help beginners master their hook grip. You may want to join a crochet support group online or find one in your locality. Sometimes one-on-one support is just the thing you need to build your confidence.

▷ Mirror Crochet

You may find sitting opposite a right-handed crocheter buddy allows you to learn a suitable hook grip.

▷ Video Support

You will find several videos demonstrating left-handed crochet skills and techniques. If you are fortunate enough to have the imaging software and know-how, you can flip the images to make them ideal for your tutoring needs.

You will find more useful tips and hints for left-handed beginners in chapter seven.

CROCHET FABRIC TENSION

Beginners sometimes find holding the hook and working the yarn tricky. Practice is essential in developing a comfortable working grip that will help to keep the tension in your crochet fabric relatively consistent and even. Keeping the yarn in a gentle, comfortable grip as you work should guarantee the thread doesn't pull too tightly and warp the crochet fabric.

Holding the Yarn

You will need patience as you learn the most effective way to control the yarn. Remember that although your style may differ from other crochet crafters, if it works for you, that's fine.

Here are several unique ways to hold your yarn. Take a look at the suggestion below to help you start your exciting crocheting journey.

▷ **Right-Handed Crocheter Yarn Hold**

Wrap the working yarn once over your left pinky finger, up under your left ring finger, and over your left forefinger.

Holding the slip knot securely but comfortably between your right middle or ring fingers and forefinger will help keep the thread moving quickly without snagging.

▷ **Left-Handed Crocheter Yarn Hold**

Years ago, left-handed crafters had to use right-handed crochet methods. Fortunately, things have changed, and left-hand crafters are now encouraged to use their unique grip to make their crocheting statements.

▷ **Essential Tips for Left-Handed Beginners**

Basically, left-handed crocheting is a mirror image of right-handed crocheting. Here are three simple, useful tips to help you keep your work aligned and recognize the RS of your project from the WS.

- Leaving the yarn tail hanging from your project will help to remind you which side of the work is facing you as you crochet. So, determine from the get-go that the yarn hangs on your left when you make the foundation chain. Thus, the WS of the fabric faces you at this stage.
- Remember to scoop the yarn clockwise every time you place the yarn over your hook.
- Although there is a definite move to support left-handed crafters with patterns, you may find a pattern you want to use, but it's written for right-handed crafters. As mentioned previously, graphs and charts should be reversed for left-handed crafters. This action is essential if your crochet project has word-specific emblems that are read from left to right.

STARTING YOUR CROCHET PROJECT

Making a slip knot is the first important step to starting your crochet project. The knot will make sure there is a solid yarn grip on the hook.

Slip Knot

Draw up about eight inches of thread from your chosen yarn, grab your crochet hook and learn to make a slip knot to hold the yarn on your hook. Although a slip knot differs from most other knot types that usually pull tight, the slip knot can smoothly slide on the crochet hook without snagging.

Also, the slip knot can easily be undone.

There are several ways in which to tie a slip knot.

▷ **Twisted Loop Method**

If you are a right-handed crafter, lay the yarn in an "n" loop on your left hand with the yarn tail closest to your thumb. Hold the yarn loop securely with your left thumb. Use your right hand to twist the working yarn once to the left so that the yarn lies over itself, leaving a large loop at the top. Make sure your left thumb secures the yarn cross-over. Push right thumb and index finger through the loop from the underside and gently grip the yarn tail, pulling it back through the loop. Use your left thumb and index finger to control the yarn movement to make sure a slip knot forms. If the slip knot has formed correctly, you should be able to adjust the knot by gently pulling the tail yarn.

▷ **Twisted "U" Method**

Lay the yarn in a U-shaped loop on your left hand with the yarn tail lying closer to your fingertips and the working yarn closer to your right thumb. Twist the working yarn once over the tail yarn to form a lasso-type loop. Pass your right thumb and index finger through the lasso loop and grab the yarn tail from below. Slowly draw the yarn back into the loop. Use your left thumb to control the yarn tail and work yarn to make sure a slip knot forms.

▷ **Over-the-Finger Wrap**

Grip the end of a suitable yarn tail length between your left thumb and index finger. Hold the end securely, wrap the working yarn clockwise once over your left index finger, and secure the yarn with your left pinkie finger. You will notice the yarn makes an "X" on your index finger. Insert the hook under the "X" and hook up the working yarn to form a loop. Slowly remove your index finger, keeping the loop over your hook. Use your left hand to adjust the knot size by pulling on the yarn to tighten the slip knot just enough that it doesn't fall off your hook.

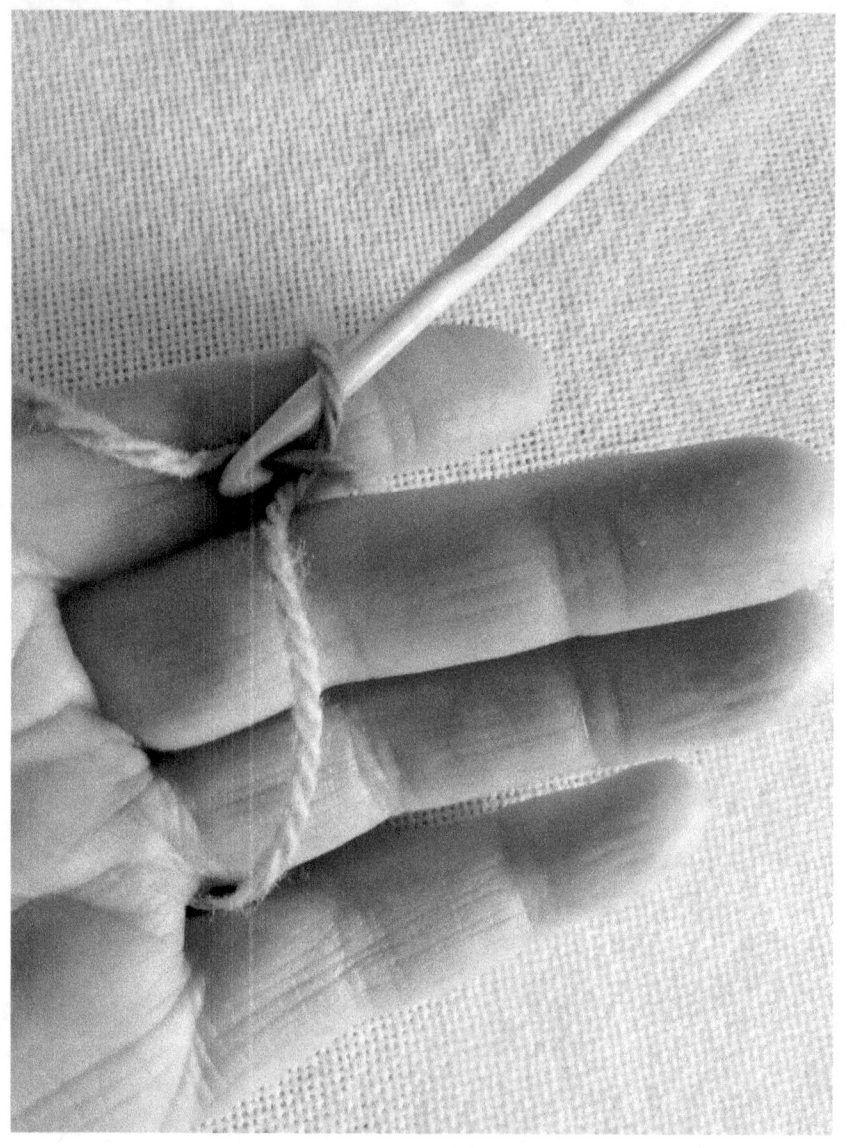

Once you have made the slip knot, loop it onto your hook and make sure it is secure without being pulled too tight.

Magic Circle

A magic circle is often used to crochet rounds. Hold your index and middle fingers together to make the circle; wrap the yarn tail to form the letter "X".

Slip your hook under the bottom yarn and hook the top yarn through.

Twist your hook, pick up the top yarn and pull it through the loop.

Then, make one chain and work the correct number of sc stitches into the magic ring.

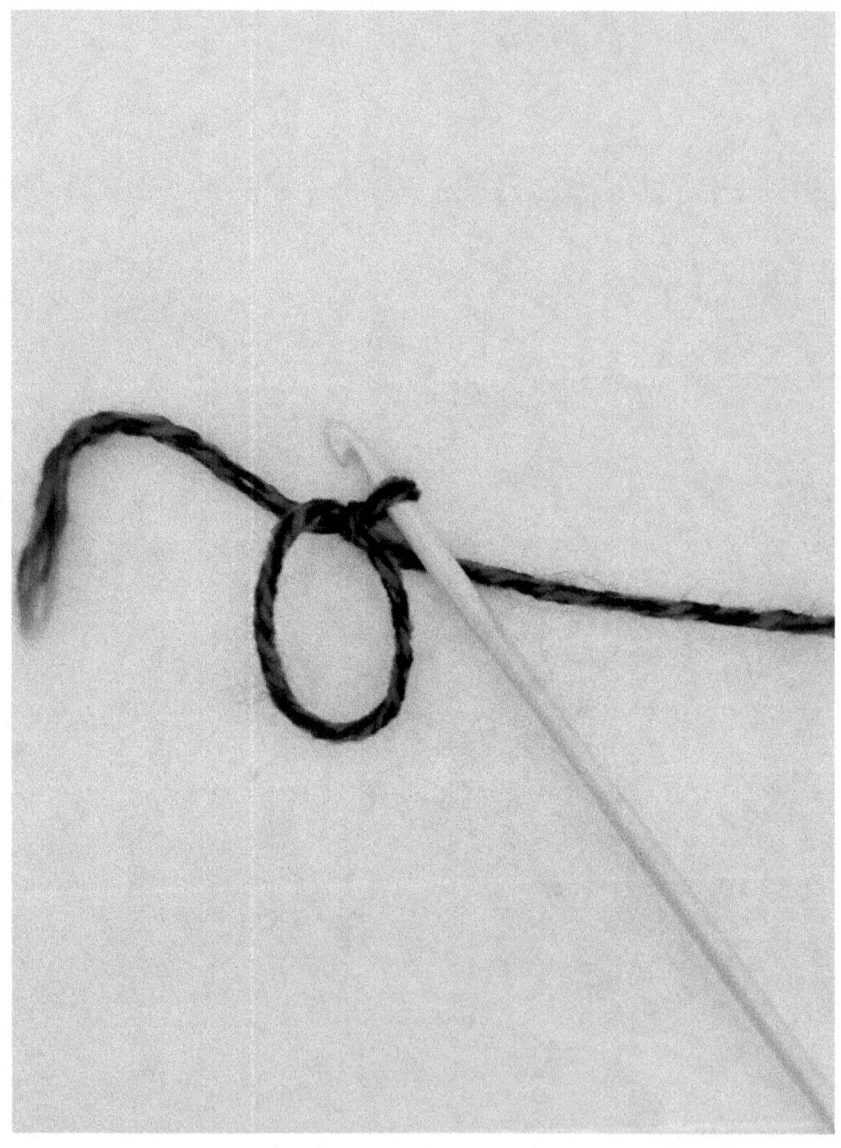

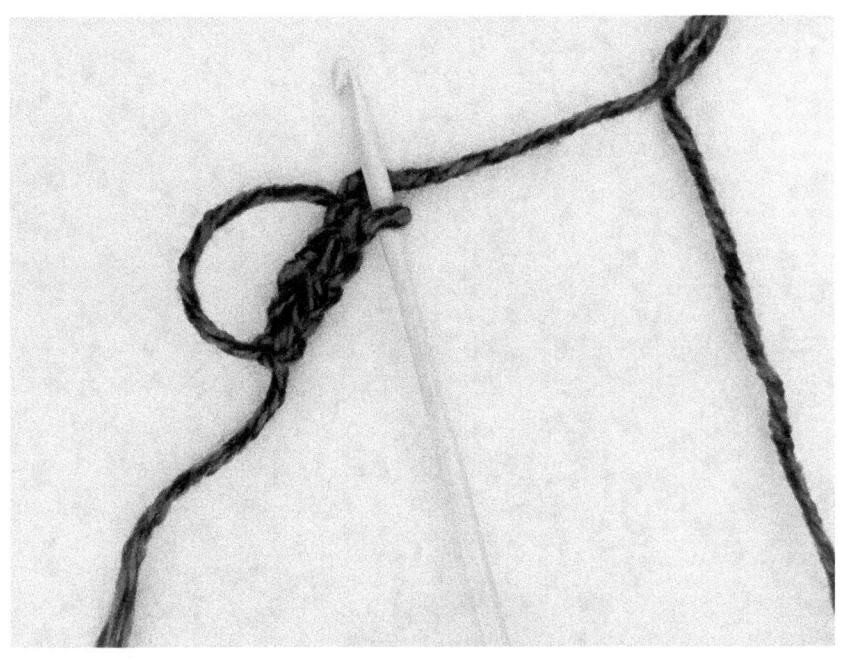

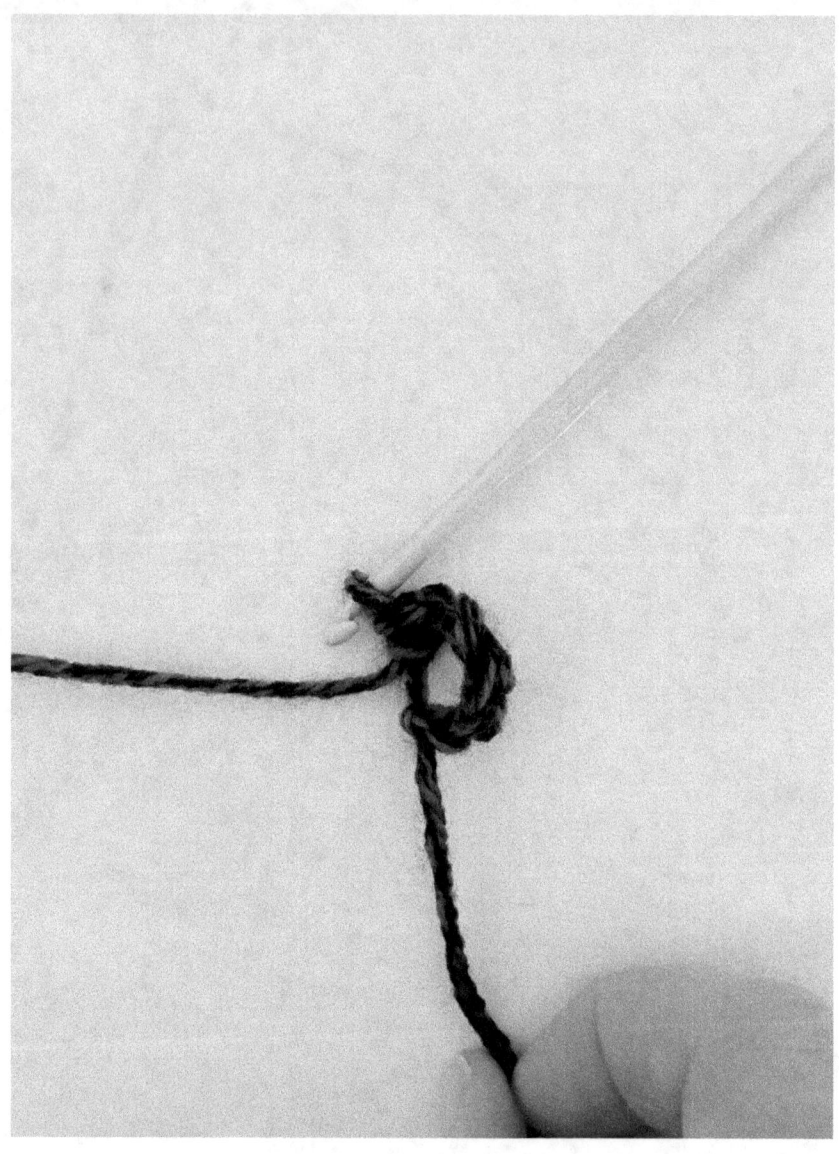

Once you have completed the number of stitches needed to start your project, work a slip stitch into the first chain and pull the yarn tail to close the magic ring.

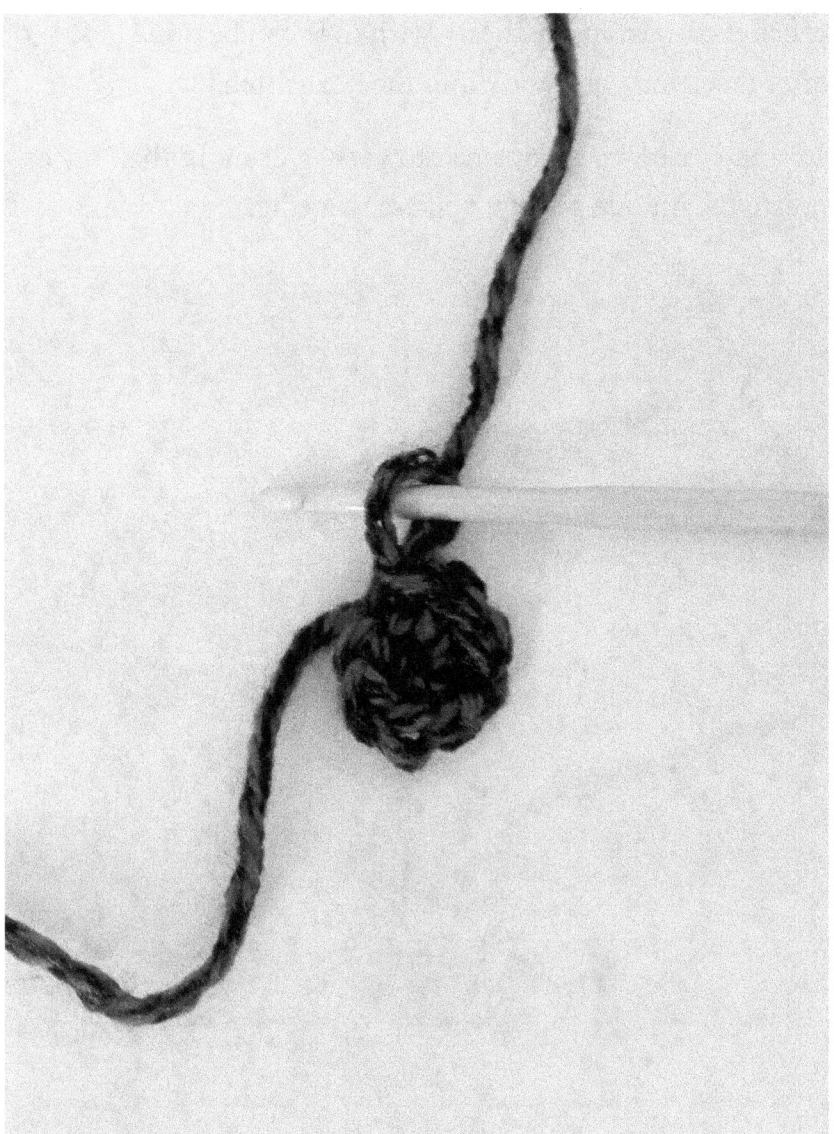

Yarn Over

Wrapping your yarn over the crochet hook is the essential step for making a new stitch. The action is termed yarn over and is designated by the abbreviation "yo". Depending on the crochet pattern instructions, yarn over can be done before or after inserting your hook into the next stitch.

In some cases, you may need to yarn over more than once to create the unique pattern you are working.

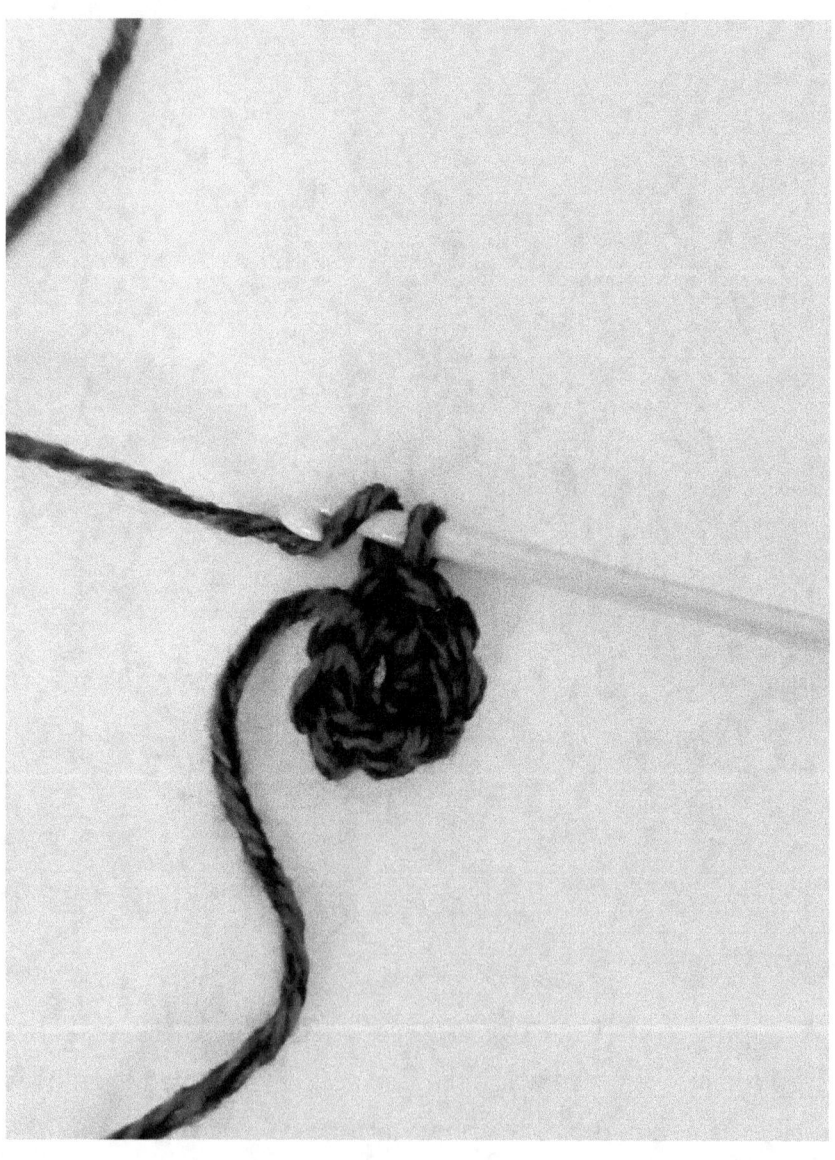

Although yarn over is a simple procedure, it's essential that you keep the yarn tension pliant and not too tight. You should be able to draw the yarn loop smoothly through the new stitch.

Foundation Chain

Starting a new crochet project is not only exciting but also brings you a sense of expectation and the desire to get started as quickly as possible. The crochet chain stitch, depicted by the abbreviation "ch", is multifunctional. It forms the foundation of all crochet projects, much like the "cast-on" row used in knitting. The chain also acts in place of stitches as a starting chain and connects stitches, creating spaces in your crochet project. Chain stitches are also used to create a decorative edge with picot stitches.

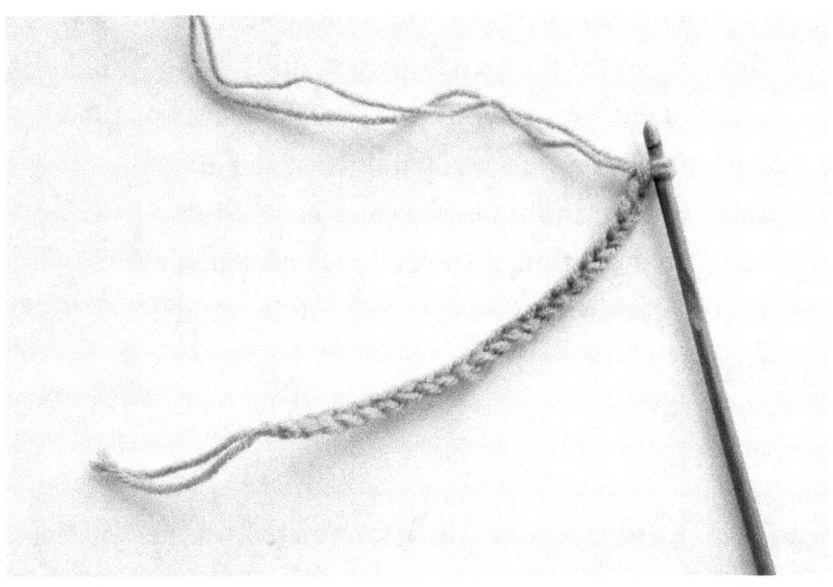

Once the slip knot is secure on the hook, loop the yarn clockwise over the hook and scoop the thread through the loop to make the first chain. Continue hooking yarn loops through until the foundation chain has the correct number of chains for your specific crochet project. Remember, the stitch on the hook is NEVER counted.

TIPS:

1. Make sure the foundation chains are not pulled too tight as you work the first pattern row along the chain. Your hook should pass comfortably through each chain without difficulty.
2. When working into the foundation chain, follow the pattern instructions. However, you can insert your hook under one or two strands of chain loops depending on the effect you want to achieve. Ideally, inserting your hook under two strands, the "v" stitch, gives a neat edge to your project. Whichever method you choose, be consistent and work all pieces the same way for multiple-piece projects.
3. Practice the action until you are confident about finding the correct hook placement in the chain stitches.

Slip Stitch (sl st)

These easy-to-make slip stitches, depicted by the abbreviation "sl st", are essential when you crochet in the round. Your pattern instructions will probably tell you to "sl st" into the starting chain to close the round, forming a chain circle. So, keeping the stitch on your hook, push the hook through the "v" stitch in the starting chain. Then loop the yarn over the hook and draw through the starting chain and the stitch on the hook. There will now be one stitch on the hook.

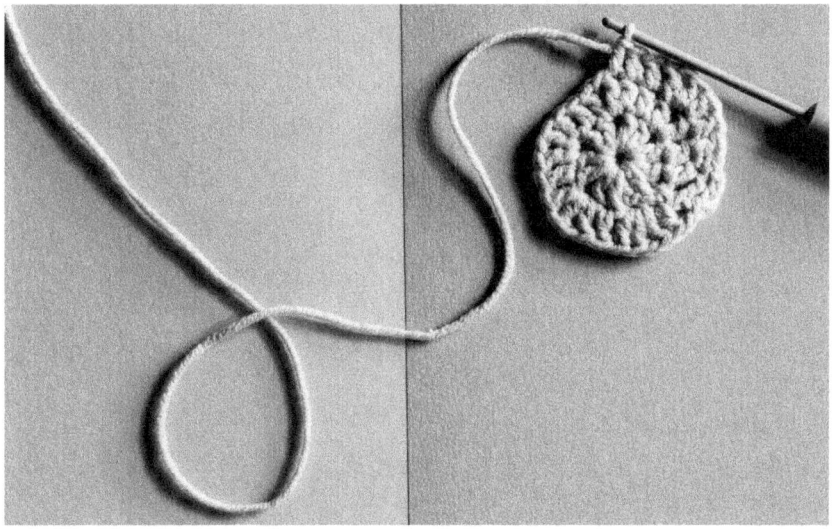

Unlike the other crochet stitches, slip stitches are not used alone to create a fabric for specific projects such as hats or afghans. The stitches are primarily used for joining two pieces of crochet fabric. They can also be used to move yarn to another project area without cutting the thread. Moreover, slip stitches can be used successfully for surface embellishments to add interest, texture, and color to a project. Finally, the stitch is used to draw yarn through a previous row.

Ways to make slip stitches

- On the foundation chain—insert your hook into the correct chain. Place the yarn over your hook and draw the thread through the loop in one fluid movement.
- In a working row—push the hook through the working stitch, yarn over, and pull the thread through the work and the loop on your hook.
- To make a chain ring—insert your hook into the first loop in the foundation chain, yarn over, and draw the thread through the first loop and the loop on your hook. The foundation chain has formed a neat ring, perfect for working in rounds.

Turning Chain

All turning chains are only worked at the start of each new row. These chains refer to the starting stitch of each new row, the height of which is determined by the number of chains you need to make. Here is an easy-to-follow guide to help you use the correct turning chain for each crochet stitch.

▷ Single Crochet

One turning chain is required when you will work single crochet along the row. Thus, the first working stitch of the pattern will be made into the second chain from the hook on the starting chain.

▷ Half Double Crochet

When working with half double crochet, you must make two turning chains. Therefore, the first stitch of your half double crochet pattern will be worked into the third chain from the hook on the starting chain.

▷ Double Crochet

The double crochet stitch needs three turning chains at the start of the first row on the foundation chain. You will then work the first double crochet into the fourth chain from the hook on the starting chain.

▷ Treble Crochet

The treble crochet stitch needs four turning chains, which means the first stitch is worked into the fifth chain from the hook on the starting chain.

You may notice stitch height increases with each crochet stitch type. The number of skipped chains also increases to make sure the row height for each unique crochet stitch remains even.

Reading a Pattern

To follow a crochet pattern, you should first know how to make the basic stitches. In addition, you must familiarize yourself with the most common pattern stitches, abbreviations, and symbols. This way, you equip yourself with the knowledge to successfully read and understand crochet patterns to produce well-crafted, neatly finished projects.

▷ **Pattern Diagrams**

Crochet crafters should read crochet diagrams in the order in which the crochet is worked. You will notice that every stitch is represented by a specific symbol to resemble its corresponding crochet stitch.

Take careful note of the position of the signs, as it indicates where you should work each stitch.

All stitch symbols are drawn and strategically laid out to create the final design as realistically as possible. Sometimes the pattern designer may emphasize specific stitches to make sure the crochet crafter places these stitches correctly in the pattern. However, the emphasized stitch sizes should be increased and then worked as expected.

▷ **Right Side (RS) and Wrong Side (WS) Rows**

▷ **Working in Rows**

Where patterns instruct you, turn your work after each row. Only the alternate rows should be worked on the right side when the work is facing you. In a crochet pattern diagram, the right side rows are usually clearly depicted in black on the chart and should be read from right to left.

Wrong side rows are many times printed in a different color, often blue, and are read from left to right.

Row numbers are usually listed at the side of the diagram and designate the beginning of the row.

▷ **Working in Rounds**

Pattern diagrams worked in rounds always have the right side of the fabric facing you. Alternate rounds worked in different stitches are color-coded in blue and black lettering.

▷ **Pattern Repeats**

In written or printed patterns, instructions that you should repeat are placed between brackets [ ] or may follow an asterisk *. Repeat the directions across the row or round, the required number of times, as instructed in the pattern. Sometimes, the repeated stitches fall short of the end of the round or row by one stitch. In this case, you will balance the row by crocheting a suitable stitch to finish the row. So, if you are working with double crochet stitches in the pattern, you will complete the row with one double crochet stitch to keep the stitch height the same as the worked row height.

▷ Gauge

Each crochet pattern gives information about the required gauge, which refers to the number of rows and stitches in a given measured area. For example, your pattern may indicate 16 stitches and five rows = four inches. When you are following a pattern for a garment, in particular, the gauge is vital for the correct size. Thus, you should use the recommended yarn weight and hook size to make sure you get the right garment size.

Before starting the actual crochet project, always work a sample to make sure you get the accurate gauge for your chosen yarn and hook size. Changing the hook size or yarn weight will alter the measurements of the finished article, and you may be disappointed with the results.

Finishing Off

Having spent time and effort on your unique crochet project, you will want to make sure you finish the crafting article neatly and securely. Depending on the purpose of the crochet article, different finishing methods can be used to secure the yarn tail and leave the fruit of your handiwork with a neat, well-finished edge and an overall professional appearance.

▷ Weave in Ends

Once your crochet project is complete, make sure you neatly weave the yarn ends into the project. Anchoring the yarn ends is vital for the ultimate success of your project. When you fasten off your thread, firmly secure the yarn tail. The overall neat appearance of the finished article gives it a professional look. It's best to work in yarn ends as carefully and invisibly as possible. Securely woven thread tails will not loosen and unravel.

▷ Neat Edging

For pillows, garments, afghans, and throws, a precise edge ensures an aesthetically pleasing finished product. You can make attractive edges in several ways. Chapter Six contains many valuable and practical ideas for plain or decorative edging.

▷ Blocking and Pressing

Some crochet projects, such as granny square jackets and crochet tablecloths made from several separate pieces, may require blocking.

Cotton Pieces

Lay the crochet pieces right side down on a padded surface, such as your ironing or fabric cutting board. For highly textured crochet fabric, lay these pieces right side down on a towel that will help ensure the bobbles are not flattened. Gently shape and stretch the fabric, making sure to do the required measurements. Secure the pieces using rust-proof pins. Dampen each piece and lightly press with a hot iron.

Do not allow the total weight of the iron to rest on the piece. Allow the pieces to cool before you remove the pins.

▷ Starching

For starched crochet pieces like doilies, pin the fabric as discussed above. Then, dab or brush the starch mixture onto the fabric using a clean sponge, brush, or small cloth. Press the fabric gently and allow it to dry before removing the pins.

Acrylic and Blended Yarn

It is seldom necessary to block fabric made from acrylic and blended yarn. However, if you feel blocking will improve the look of the garment or fabric, place the pattern pieces right side facing down on a padded surface and secure each, as discussed above. Dampen but DO NOT PRESS. Once dry, the fabric pieces should hold their shape sufficiently well to be attached to your project.

Joining Seams

Seaming your completed crochet pieces need not be the chore you may think. Believe it or not, choosing to join your fabric pieces plays a vital role in the finished product's appearance, functionality, and overall design.

Making the seaming process part of your project's overall success will ensure you have a finished product of which you can feel proud.

There are several ways to join your crochet fabric pieces. Always choose the best finishing method for the project. For example, you may want the seams on your unique granny square rug to add interest. Thus, you will make sure the seams are visible for an added decorative appearance.

TIPS:

1. Always count the edge stitches in the two pieces of crochet fabric to be joined. You will find it challenging to join uneven project pieces. Thus, if you have granny squares, each square should have the same number of stitches as every other square you have crocheted for the project.

2. To give your squares a neat, professional edge, consider adding a row of single crochet to each.

▷ Visible Seams

Visible seams are usually worked on the right side in a contrasting color. Place the wrong sides together (of the pieces to be joined) and secure with pins. Using the yarn of your choice, attach the parts using an attractive stitch from one of the suggestions below.

- **Whip Stitch**—working with the wrong sides of the fabric together, make sure the edges are even. Secure the fabric using non-rust pins. Using a yarn needle and thread or yarn of your choice, work a tiny back stitch into where the inner seam is proposed to be. Push the needle through the top fabric piece. Place the needle into the lower fabric piece and push it up through the top piece again, ensuring the yarn loops over the edges of both fabric pieces. Repeat the sewing action to create a series of evenly spaced and similarly sized loops along the seam length. End with a tiny back stitch between the fabric pieces or weave the yarn tail securely into the fabric so it will not quickly come loose.
- **Cross Stitch**—similar to whip stitch, cross stitch consists of two stitching rows. Using a longer thread, follow the whip stitch instructions but do not fasten off the yarn when you reach the fabric piece's end.

Turn and work back, crossing each stitch to create an "x" until you reach the starting point. Weave the yarn neatly and secure it well.

- **Crochet Seam**—place the pieces to be joined, right sides together. Using your hook and contrasting yarn, slip stitch through the bottom right corners. Pull up a loop and make a chain. Then, single crochet through both pieces of fabric along the entire seam. Make sure the stitches are not pulled too tightly, or the fabric is likely to pucker. Repeat the crochet seaming process until your project is complete. Finally, finish off with an attractive edging of your choice. The border works particularly well on throws, blankets, and scarf edges.

There are many other ways to attach crochet pieces, some of which involve specific crochet stitches for which you will use a hook instead of a yarn needle. Once you have mastered the exciting array of stitches discussed in Chapter Six, you may want to experiment with using one of these as a joining method.

▷ **Invisible Seams**

When attaching pieces for a garment, or a delicate, attractive tablecloth, you will want to make invisible seams that will work on the wrong side of the fabric.

- **Mattress Stitch**—working with two pieces of crochet fabric, lay them side-by-side, right sides up. Using a matching thread and yarn needle, insert the needle through the bottom right corner of the crochet piece on the right side. Draw the thread up and secure it with a tiny back stitch or a knot. Work vertically through the next stitch on the right side. Insert the needle into the bottom left corner and up through the next stitch on the left. Then, insert the needle into the second stitch on the right, and work vertically through the next stitch. Repeat the same stitch on the left. Continue working along both edges until the join is complete. Finish off with a neat knot or secure back stitch.

- **Invisible Seaming**—to make an invisible join, you will need to use identical yarn for your crochet project. Place the crochet pieces with right sides together and secure them with non-rust pins. The invisible seam works well if the project pieces have a sufficiently long yarn tail that can be used for joining.

- **Slip Stitching**—with the right sides of the fabric together, using a yarn needle and working from right to left, make a small back stitch and slip stitch through alternating loops from one piece to the other until both are securely attached. Finish off with a tiny back stitch and weave the yarn tail out of sight. The invisible seam can successfully use a hook to slip-stitch the crochet fabric pieces together.

THE KEY TAKEAWAY

Now that you have some understanding of the basics of crochet craft, you are ready to grow your crochet knowledge and skills. Let's dive into the next chapter, which introduces you to various crochet stitches. You will also find easy, step-by-step instructions for making each stitch, which is essential for creating a wide variety of unique and fascinating projects.

WHAT ARE YOUR THOUGHTS?

Are you enjoying the book?
Have you learned something new?
Has it helped you improve your crochet skills?
Will you recommend it to others?

Let me and your fellow crocheters know by leaving your review on Amazon!
Please scan the QR code below or visit the link to **Leave a Review**:

https://www.amazon.com/review/create-review/?asin=
B0BDXK94N2

By leaving your review, you are helping to make this book successful, and by doing that, helping others learn and improve their crochet skills and creativity!

Thank you very much

-Genevieve

DIFFERENT STITCHES A PROJECT MAY USE

C rochet is an easy-to-learn handcraft. With a sound knowledge of several basic stitches, you will be ready to create unique, trendy, and beautiful items for friends, family, and your home.

ESSENTIAL CROCHET STITCHES

In this chapter, you will find several basic beginner stitches and some super-useful tips to help you on your way to crocheting success. You will also find a few easy-to-crochet projects to build your skills and confidence.

You will already have mastered the essential slip knot and foundation chain discussed in Chapter Five. Now you are ready to begin your crochet project.

CROCHET STITCH ABBREVIATION CHART

For ease of reference, many crochet patterns use specific symbols to depict the different stitches. The chart below is helpful for beginner crochet crafters in learning to identify these symbols and understand their instructions.

Symbol	Abbr.	US Stitch	UK Stitch	Formation	Turning Chain
⬭	CH	Chain	Chain (ch)	Insert hook, YO, draw loop through loop on hook	
⬤	SLST	Slip Stitch	Slip Stitch (sl)	Insert hook through stitch, YO, draw loop through chain stitch and loop on hook	
†	SC	Single Crochet	Double Crochet (dc)	Insert hook through stitch, YO, draw loop back through stitch (2 loops on hook), YO, draw through both loops on hook	1
T	HDC	Half Double Crochet	Half Treble Crochet (htr)	YO, insert hook through stitch, YO, draw loop back through stitch (3 loops on hook), YO, pull loop through all 3 loops on hook	2
⊤	DC	Double Crochet	Treble Crochet (tr)	YO, insert hook through stitch, YO, draw loop through stitch (3 loops on hook), YO, draw through 2 loops on hook (2 loops on hook), YO, draw through last 2 loops	3
⊥	TR	Treble Crochet	Double Treble Crochet (dtr)	YO twice, insert hook through stitch, YO, draw loop through stitch (4 loops on hook), YO, draw through 2 loops (3 loops on hook), YO, draw through 2 loops (2 loops on hook), YO, draw through last 2 loops	4
⊥	DTR	Double Treble Crochet	Triple Treble Crochet (ttr)	YO three times, insert hook through stitch, YO, draw loop through stitch (5 loops on hook), YO, draw loop through 2 loops (4 loops on hook), YO, draw loop through 2 loops (3 loops on hook) YO, draw loop through 2 loops (2 loops on hook), YO, draw through last 2 loops	5

Single Crochet (sc)

Now that you have mastered the chain and slip stitches that form the first two steps of most crochet projects, you are ready to learn the single crochet stitch, designated by the abbreviation "sc".

Many patterns use single crochet, a short stitch creating a close-weave fabric. Changing your hook size and yarn weight will allow you to create various densities.

The simplest crochet stitch, single crochet, is easy and quick for making rows or rounds. To create stunning, unique projects, you can experiment with different crochet stitch combinations.

Here's how to do the single crochet, the first stitch you will need for many crochet projects.

- To start a flat project, crochet a foundation chain of the required length. Twelve chains should be enough for practicing the single crochet stitch for sample purposes.
- Insert your hook under the "v" of the second chain from the starting chain. The chain on the hook acts as the first single crochet in the row. *Yarn over the hook, draw up a loop to make two loops on your hook. Again, yarn over and pull through both loops, leaving one loop on the hook**.
- Repeat from * to ** until the row ends.

You have completed a row of single crochet stitches that makes a neat edge for starting and ending rows for blankets, throws, and washcloths.

Single crochet is ideal for closely woven tote bags; gorgeous Amigurumi stand-alone, stuffed, three-dimensional projects, and tiny toys. The stitch is also suitable for elegant flap clutch bags, beanies, snug baby blankets, washcloths, slippers, and hair accessories.

Helpful Hints

- Once you reach the end of each row, count the stitches to make sure you have the required number. Although you may feel counting stitches at the end of every row is a waste of time, rest assured the process will make sure your work remains even and does not warp.
- If you are missing a stitch at the end of the row, for example, there are 16 instead of 17 stitches, pick up

the last stitch from the end of the previous row before turning.

- There is only ONE turning chain when you are working on single crochet projects.

Half Double Stitch (hdc)

Half double, abbreviated "hdc", is the second crochet stitch, which you will find helpful in many crafty crochet projects you want to finish quickly. A beautiful and straightforward foundation stitch, the half double crochet stitch has an added unique third loop that changes the stitch height. In addition, the stitch builds on the single crochet stitch by adding another step.

You will find the half double stitch in a variety of crafty crochet projects. And, unless you are using a specific pattern that details the exact materials you need, you can use any hook size and suitable yarn to create many unique items. Check the yarn label for hook size details.

Ideally, half double crochet projects have a looser weave than those using the single crochet. Therefore, the height of the half double crochet stitch is slightly taller than the single crochet and somewhat shorter than the double crochet stitch.

Here's how to make this attractive, adaptable stitch, which may quickly become a favorite in your crochet stitch collection.

- To start a flat project, crochet a foundation chain of the required length. For sample purposes, thirteen chains should be enough for practicing the half double crochet stitch.
- To make the first "hdc", loop the yarn over your hook and insert the hook into the "v" of the third chain on the starting chain. Now, draw up a loop. This action starts the first stitch in the row. Notice the height of the stitch. You should have three loops on your hook.
- Then, *yarn over again and pull the thread through all three loops.
- *Yarn over your hook and insert your hook into the next stitch. Draw the thread through all three stitches.
- Repeat from * to the end of the row.

Helpful Hints

- Once again, count the stitches in each row to make sure you have the required number.
- If you are missing a stitch at the end of the row, pick up and work the last stitch from the end of the previous row before turning.
- There are TWO turning chains when you are working half double crochet projects.

You have completed a row of half double crochet stitches. Notice that these stitches are slightly taller than their single crochet cousins.

Half double crochet is ideal for gorgeous ribbed beanies, scarves, and wrist warmers. Stitches can also be used for cozy throws and colorful blankets. In addition, the half double crochet stitch is sometimes used for beautifully detailed sweaters and is ideal for textured bags.

Double Crochet (dc)

One of the basic stitches, double crochet, is depicted by the abbreviation "dc". Double crochet is one of the most favored stitches used by crochet crafters. It offers a firm, attractive surface, giving your projects a professional finish. Once again, double crochet builds on the half double stitch but adds an extra step.

- To start a flat project, crochet a foundation chain of the required length. Make a crochet sample using 14 chains to practice double crochet.
- Yarn over, and insert the hook under the "v" of the fourth chain from your hook. The three chains on your hook form the first double crochet. Now, scoop up one loop. You should have three loops on your hook.
- Yarn over and draw through the first two loops. There are two loops left on the hook. Yarn over again and draw through the last two loops.

- Then, *yarn over, slip the hook under the "v" of the next stitch, and pull up a loop. Finally, yarn over and draw the thread through two loops, leaving two loops on the hook.
- Yarn over again and pull the thread through these two loops.
- Repeat from * to the row's end.

Helpful Hints

- Once again, count the stitches in each row to make sure you have the required number.
- If you are missing a stitch at the end of the row, pick up and work the last double crochet stitch into the end of the previous row before turning.
- There are THREE turning chains when you are working on double crochet projects.

Your first row of double crochet stitches is complete. Note the height of the stitches compared to the half double crochet and single crochet stitches above. The comparison will help you recognize these stitches in a pattern.

The double crochet stitch is ideal for granny squares (below) or the super-attractive V-stitch you will find farther down the list of stitches discussed here.

Treble Crochet

Treble crochet, depicted by the abbreviation "tr", is four chains high. Projects using treble crochet work up quickly to create attractive, openwork, lacy effects.

Ideal for loose blankets and flowing summery swimwear cover-ups, treble crochet holds its own amongst favorite crochet stitch choices.

Once you have mastered double crochet, you should find treble crochet easy enough. Like its predecessor, treble crochet involves an extra yarn-over to make the stitch taller than its double crochet companion. The basic crochet motions are the same. Thus, learning the treble stitch improves your crochet skills. You will likely discover working with taller stitches opens a new dimension to crochet projects. The taller stitches are ideal for projects with larger spaces in the fabric weave.

Here's how to crochet the quick and easy treble stitch.

- To start a flat project, crochet a foundation chain of the required length. For sample purposes, 15 chains should be enough for practicing the treble crochet stitch.
- Wrap the yarn twice around the hook. Insert the hook into the fifth stitch from the hook on the starting chain and yarn over. Pull up the loop. There should be four loops on your hook that form the first treble stitch in the row.
- Yarn over again. Draw the yarn through two loops. There should be three loops remaining on the hook.
- Yarn over again. Draw the yarn through two loops. There should now be two loops.
- Yarn over once again. Draw the yarn through the two loops, leaving one loop on the hook. You have completed the first treble crochet.
- Now, for the second treble crochet stitch, *wrap the yarn three times over your hook and insert the hook

into the next stitch. Yarn over again. There should be four loops on the hook.

- Yarn over again. Draw the yarn through two loops. There should be three loops remaining on the hook.
- Yarn over again. Draw the yarn through two loops. There should now be two loops.
- Yarn over once again. Draw the yarn through the two loops, leaving one loop on the hook**.
- Repeat from * to ** until the end of the row.

Helpful Hints

- Count the stitches in each row to make sure you have the required number.
- Adjust the stitch number by adding an extra treble crochet stitch into the last treble crochet stitch at the end of the previous row before turning.
- There are FOUR turning chains when you are working on treble crochet projects.

You have completed your first row of treble crochet stitches. Compare the height of the treble crochet stitches to the double crochet variety. You will see the stitch height increase to four stitches high.

At the end of every treble crochet row, turn and make four chains to make sure each row is the same height as the treble crochet stitches.

Treble crochet makes it the ideal stitch for creating attractive cables and a basket weave effect.

Double Treble Crochet

The double treble stitch, designated the abbreviation "dtr", is also called double triple and is one step up from treble crochet. The longer stitch is often used in specific designs requiring taller stitches for visual effect.

Let's look at how the stitch is made.

- Yarn three times over the hook. Then, insert the hook into the sixth stitch from the starting chain.
- Yarn over and draw the thread through the stitch. There should be five loops on the hook.
- Yarn over the hook. Then, draw the thread through two loops. There should now be four loops on the hook.
- Yarn over again and draw the thread through two loops. There are now three loops remaining on the hook.
- Yarn over again and draw the thread through two loops. There should be two loops on the hook.
- Yarn over for the final time. Draw the thread through the remaining two loops to complete one double treble crochet.

Helpful Hints

- Count the stitches in each row to make sure you have the required number. Adjust as needed by picking up the last stitch in the previous row and working a double treble stitch before turning.
- There are FIVE turning chains when you are working on double treble crochet projects.

Triple Treble Crochet

The tallest stitch is the triple treble, designated by the abbreviation "trtr". Although tall stitches have unique features, they are created much the same way as the other crochet stitches. The only difference is that a few extra steps are required to complete each tall stitch.

The triple treble can be used when you especially need high stitching for attractive, stylish scarves and lightweight, breathable blankets. Triple treble crochet is also used for interesting curtaining effects.

Here's how to crochet the fast, effective triple treble stitch.

- Loop the yarn over the hook four times.
- Insert the hook into the seventh chain from the hook.
- Yarn over and draw the thread through two loops. There should be six loops on the hook.
- *Yarn over the hook again and draw the thread through two loops**. There are now five loops left on the hook.
- Repeat the instructions * to ** three times until one loop is on the hook.

The triple treble stitch is now complete.

Helpful Hints

- Count the stitches in each row to make sure you have the required number. Adjust as needed by picking up the last stitch in the previous row and working a triple treble stitch before turning.
- There are SIX turning chains when working on triple treble crochet projects.

INCREASING AND DECREASING

Most crochet project instructions stipulate whether you should work through each stitch's back or front loops. However, where no clear instructions are given, always work under the two strands, v-stitch, of the top stitch in the row below. Learning to increase and decrease stitches is vital for the success of many crochet projects.

Increasing

To increase the width of your crochet fabric, two or more stitches are worked into one stitch periodically across the row, to make sure of an even fabric finish. All crochet stitches, from single to triple treble, are increased similarly.

For example, increasing in single crochet is needed in Amigurumi projects.

Work on a foundation chain of fourteen chains.

Row 1: Make one chain, and work one single crochet into the second chain from the hook. Then, work one single crochet into each chain across the row. Turn.

Row 2: Make one chain and *work single crochet into the first three stitches. Then, work two single crochet into the fourth stitch. Repeat from * to the end of the row, and finish with one single crochet. You should have sixteen stitches.

Decreasing

The abbreviation for the decrease is written as "sc2tog" (single crochet), "hdc2tog" (half double crochet), etc.

Reducing the width of your crochet fabric is done by working two or more stitches together, leaving the last loop of each stitch on the hook, and then pulling the thread through all the remaining loops to leave one loop on the hook.

▷ **Single Crochet**

For example, working in single crochet, draw up a loop in two consecutive stitches to decrease. There will be three loops on your hook. Yarn over and draw the thread through all three loops.

▷ **Double Crochet**

Decreasing in double crochet is a little more complicated. Work one double crochet as follows: Yarn over, insert your hook into the first stitch, yarn over and pull the thread through two loops. There should be two loops left on your hook. Now, yarn over, insert your hook into the second stitch, and pull up a loop. You should now have four loops on your hook. Yarn over, pull the thread through two loops, leaving three loops on the hook. Yarn over again and pull through all three loops.

Although the increasing and decreasing processes may seem confusing initially, practice these skills before embarking on patterns with these instructions. It's easier to mess up a small swatch of crochet fabric than your prized masterpiece!

STITCH VARIATIONS

The wonderful thing about crochet is the versatility of the stitches. Many variations are made up of basic stitch combinations, so once you have mastered the basics, you embark on an exciting crochet adventure that will bring you hours of pleasure, and you will delight your family and friends with your beautiful, unique crochet projects.

Shells

Groups of completed crochet stitches worked together into the same stitch are often called shells. The fan-shaped effect of these stitches creates an attractive design in many crochet projects.

Sometimes shells are used as a method of increasing stitches, to good effect. Most crocheted shells are worked using the longer stitches such as half double crochet, double crochet, treble, and triple treble crochet, as these stitches lend themselves to a more significant effect in shell designs.

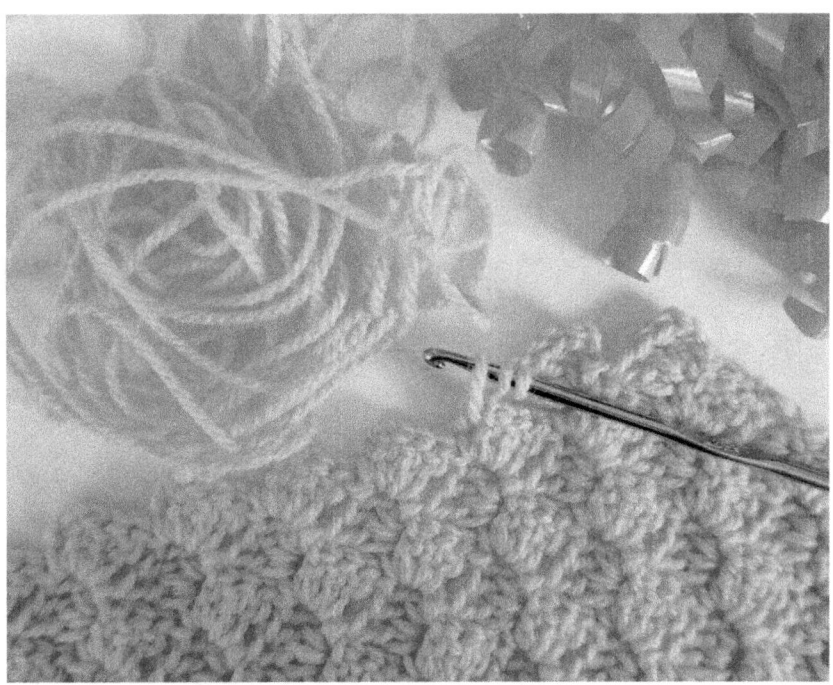

Clusters

The exciting thing about crocheting clusters is that you can successfully join combinations of chosen stitches to create attractive designs. The best method for making clusters is leaving the last loop of each stitch on the hook until you have worked the number of stitches you need for the group.

The most important thing about clusters is that you must carefully read the pattern to make sure you understand where to insert the hook into each cluster's leg. Sometimes cluster legs are worked into adjacent stitches, while at other times, stitches are skipped between cluster legs.

Ideally, like crochet shells, most clusters also work in the longer stitches for a more significant effect.

Bobbles

When a crochet cluster is worked into one stitch, a distinctive bobble shape forms. The bobbles form a delightful, attractive textured surface for your crochet projects. Crochet bobbles are usually produced with double crochet and longer stitches.

Popcorns

Similar to bobbles, popcorns are made from completed groups of stitches worked into a single stitch. Popcorns are folded and closed at the top by an extra chain. The stitches are easy-to-work, effective, and eye-catching in any crochet project. Popcorns are usually worked with double crochet and longer stitches.

Puff Stitch

Like bobbles, puff stitches are also worked into a single stitch using half double crochet stitches. However, because the half double crochet is shorter than other stitches, the puff stitch can only be closed when the required number of puff stitches have been made.

Filet Crochet

This type of crochet is usually worked from intricate stitch diagrams or graphic patterns and consists of networking the background in double crochet and chains.

Filet charts are read from top to bottom. Right-side rows are interpreted from right to left, and wrong-side rows are read in the opposite direction from left to right. Every open square designates a space, and each filled-in block represents a stitch or group of stitches, depending on the pattern.

Every row in the filet crochet starts with three chains, which always count as one double crochet.

Keeping the filet pattern balanced and correct can be challenging, but if you mark completed rows as you go, you will soon get the hang of this gorgeous, timeless crochet style.

WORKING IN ROUNDS

Motifs are usually worked in rounds rather than rows. Each round starts at a central point or ring and works outwards towards the rim. Always keep the right side facing you when working in rounds. This action applies to other patterns such as Amigurumi, crocheted hats, socks, and circular washcloths.

The central ring is usually made by working the required number of chains and slip stitching the last chain into the first. Then, one or more chains are worked at the start of every round to make sure of the correct stitch height. So, if you are working in double crochet, you will make three chains at the beginning of every round.

All the stitches worked in the first round are placed into the center of the ring, creating a wheel shape of crochet stitches. At the end of each round, make a slip stitch to close the round.

Working the second and subsequent rounds, chain three and insert your hook under the v-stitch of each stitch in the previous round.

To keep rounds from buckling, regular increasing is needed. For example, you may be instructed to work two double crochet stitches into every fourth stitch in round three.

At the end of the final round, slip stitch to complete the round before fastening off by making one chain. Snip the yarn and pull through to form a neat knot.

LEARNING SPECIFIC CROCHET STITCHES

Now the fun begins! Having learned the basics of crochet, you are ready to extend your crochet skills and jump into the wonderful, creative world of crochet stitches to make unique, breathtaking projects of your own.

Granny Stripe Stitch

Consisting of three basic stitches—he double crochet, the single crochet, and the slip stitch—the attractive, easy-to-master granny stripe stitch is ideal for those colorful, eye-catching throws to keep you snug during the chilly season.

V-Double Crochet Stitch

Ideal for lovely afghans and throws, the v-double crochet stitch creates attractive Vs across the crochet project.

To start your v-double crochet project, chain an even number of stitches for the width of your intended project.

Row 1: Double crochet into the fourth chain from the hook. *Skip one chain and make two double crochet into the next chain**. Repeat *...** to complete the row. Turn.

Row 2: Chain three and make one double crochet into the first chain space next to the three chains. Then, *skip one chain space and make two double crochets into the space between the two double crochet clumps in the previous row**. Repeat *...** for the rest of the row. You will notice the attractive "v" pattern developing.

Row 3 onward: Repeat row two as many times as needed.

Finish the project with a row of single crochet stitches to give a neat edge.

The beauty of the v-double crochet stitch lies in your color choice. You can change the yarn color at the end of every row or work two to three rows in each color. After that, it's entirely up to your unique ideas.

Moss Stitch

Ideal for beginners, the moss stitch, also known as granite or linen stitch, is created by the successive use of two basic crochet stitches: a chain stitch followed by single crochet.

The attractive effect of the moss stitch is ideal for scarves, shawls, and cowls. In addition, the stitch is great for blankets, throws, and even sweaters.

Here's how to do this fascinating crochet stitch.

Important: There are two chains at the start of each row, which counts as one moss stitch. Start by chaining an even number of stitches to suit the length or width of the item you want to make—a scarf or knee rug are ideal starter projects.

Row 1: Work one single crochet into the second chain. [chain one and make a single crochet into the next chain]—repeat the [...] to the end of the row finishing with single crochet. Turn.

Row 2: Chain two, single crochet into the first chain space, [chain one, skip one stitch, make a single crochet into the next chain space]—repeat the [...] to the end of the row finishing with single crochet. Turn.

Row 3: Chain two, single crochet into the first chain space, [chain one, skip one stitch, single crochet into the next chain space]—repeat the [...] to the end of the row, finishing with single crochet. Turn.

Row 4—end: Repeat row three until you reach the required length.

When crocheting larger projects, you may want to change the yarn color as you work on different project sections.

Here are the simple, easy-to-follow steps to get the best color change results.

- Leaving two loops on the hook at the end of a row, wrap the next color yarn over the hook and draw it through the loops. Pull the tail-end of the previous color yarn to secure the new yarn color.
- Turn your work, crochet two chains, and continue with the moss stitch pattern.

Star Stitch

The attractive, dense, starburst shape is perfect for thick winter blankets especially suited for a child's room. Also known as "daisy stitch," the star stitch row is formed by spikes followed by a row of half double crochet.

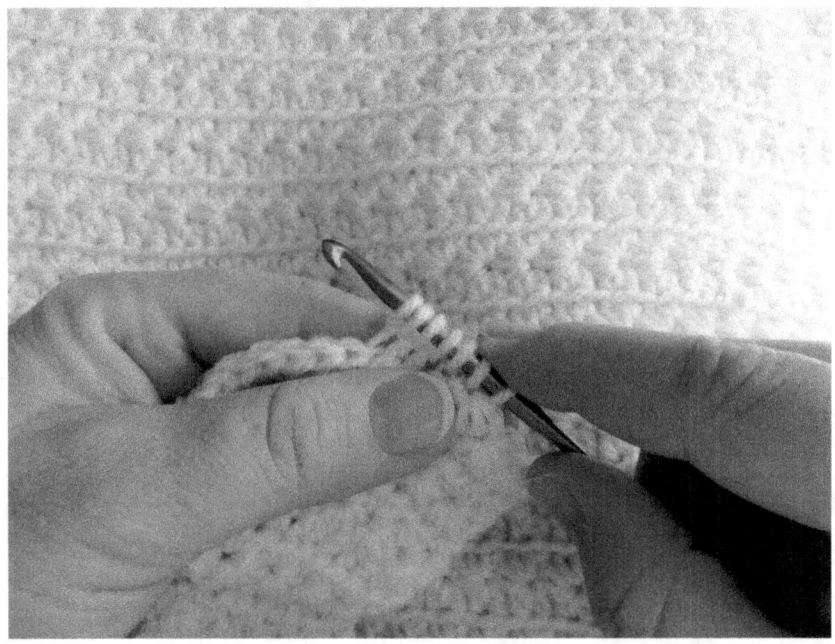

Follow the step-by-step instructions here to learn the beautiful star stitch. Make an odd number of chains. Then, work carefully to make sure you follow the stitching to make the perfect star.

Row 1:

First Star: Insert the hook into the second chain, yarn over, and draw up a loop. Leaving the loop on the hook, insert the hook into the next chain, yarn over and draw up a loop. There are three loops on your hook. Continue in this manner until you have six loops on your hook. Keep the yarn tension loose and make sure all the loops are the same size. Now, yarn over again, pull the thread through all six loops, and chain one to create the attractive star shape.

Second Star: *Insert your hook into the center (eye) of the first star. Yarn over and pull through. There are two loops on the hook. Insert the hook between the last two spikes of the first star, yarn over, and draw up the third loop on the hook. Next, insert your hook into the last stitch of the previous star, yarn over, and draw up the fourth loop. Insert the hook into the next chain, yarn over, and pull up the fifth loop. And again into the following chain, yarn over and draw up the sixth loop. Now, yarn over and pull through all six loops for the first star. Chain one to finish the second star**.

Third Star, onwards. Repeat *...** until the end of the first line. Finish the row with a star. Turn.

Row 2:

Chain two and work one half double crochet into the first stitch after the chain. Then work one half double crochet into the eye of the star in the previous row. Work another double crochet into the next stitch and one double crochet into the eye of the second star in the previous row. Work one double crochet into the next stitch and another double crochet into the eye of the third star in the previous row, until the end of the row, finishing with one double crochet. Turn.

Row 3:

Chain three, insert your hook into the base of the chain on the hook, yarn over, and pull through. There are two loops on the hook. Insert the hook into the next chain, yarn over, and draw up the third loop. Continue until there are six loops on your hook. Then, yarn over, and pull through all six loops together. Chain one to finish the first star in the new row, which in this case is row three.

Second star: *Insert the hook into the eye of the first star, yarn over and pull up a loop. Then, insert the hook between the last two spikes of the first star, yarn over, and draw up the third loop on the hook. Next, insert your hook into the last stitch of the previous star, yarn over, and draw up the fourth loop. Insert the hook into the next chain, yarn over, and pull up the fifth loop. And again into the following chain, yarn over and draw up the sixth loop. Now, yarn over and pull through all six loops for the first star. Chain one to finish the second star**.

Third Star, onwards. Repeat *...** until the end of the first line. Finish the row with a star. Turn.

Row 4: Repeat row two.

Row 5: Repeat row three.

Finish the project with the half double crochet row to make sure a neat, straight edge.

Puff Stitch

If you want to add a touch of pizzazz to a crochet project, why not try the fun-to-work puff stitch? Adding glamour and gorgeous texture, this unique stitch is super-easy. The double-sided bobbles work up, as the name suggests, into soft, attractive puffs. A puff stitch is a variation of half double crochet in which extra loops are added. It is a very effective stitch for textured projects, including glamorous scarves, snug blankets, trendy sweaters, and hats.

Row 1:

First Puff Stitch: Crochet an even number of chains. Yarn over and insert your crochet hook into chain 4. Put the yarn over the hook. Pull up a loop. There are three loops on your hook. Now, yarn over your hook, insert the hook into the same chain stitch, and pull up a loop. *Then, yarn over your hook, insert the hook into the same chain stitch, and pull up a loop**. There should be five stitches on your hook. Now, repeat *...** once more. There should now be seven loops on the hook. Yarn over and pull the yarn through all the loops on your hook. Make one chain to secure the puff.

Second Puff Stitch: *Skip one chain, yarn over, insert the hook into the next chain, yarn over and pull up a loop. Yarn over again, insert the hook into the same chain and pull up a loop, yarn over again and pull up another loop. Yarn over and pull the thread through all seven loops. Work one chain**. Repeat *...** to the end of the row.

Row 2: Make three chains, yarn over, insert the hook into the chain space between the two puff stitches in the previous row and draw up a loop. Yarn over your hook, insert the hook into the same chain space, and draw up another loop. Yarn over your hook, insert the hook into the same chain space, and pull up a loop. There should be seven loops on your hook. Now, yarn over and pull the thread through the seven loops. Make one chain to complete the first puff stitch of the second row. Continue working puffs into the chain spaces between the puff stitches on the previous row, finishing with a puff stitch. Turn.

Row 3 to last: Repeat row 2 until the required length is reached.

Cluster Stitch

Ideal for creating a thick fabric, the cluster stitch uses the single crochet stitch, which is ideal for beginners to quickly master.

For the test sample, start with 13 chain stitches.

Row 1:

Cluster 1: Insert your hook into the second chain from the hook, yarn over, and draw up a loop. Push your hook into the following chain, yarn over your hook, and draw up the third loop. Insert the hook into the next chain, yarn over, and pull up the fourth loop. Yarn over and draw the thread through all four loops. Work one chain to secure the cluster.

Insert the hook into the next chain, yarn over, and pull up a loop. Insert the hook into the following chain, yarn over, and draw up a loop. Insert the hook into the next chain, yarn over, and pull up the fourth loop. Yarn over and draw the thread through all four loops. Work one chain to secure the cluster. Continue making single crochet clusters until the end of the row. Finish with a single crochet. Turn.

Row 2: Chain one, insert the hook in the first stitch and draw up a loop. Insert your hook into the next stitch, and draw up a loop. Insert your hook in the following stitch and pull up the fourth loop. Yarn over and draw it through all four loops. Repeat until the row's end. Finish with a single crochet. Turn your work.

Row 3: Repeat row 2 until the required length is reached.

Waistcoat Stitch

This simple stitch is made with single crochet to create flat, closely woven fabric ideal for waistcoats, hats, and fingerless mittens. The secret to success with the waistcoat stitch is to work into the posts instead of the stitch loops.

Waistcoat stitch lends itself better to working in rounds, thus keeping the right side facing you as you work. It's also easier to insert your hook into the correct spot, between the v-stitch, when working on the right side only.

For the trial sample, make 10 chain stitches.

Round 1: Missing the first chain, work single crochet stitches along the entire row. Turn.

Round 2: Chain one and make one single crochet into the v-stitch between the post legs of the stitch in the row below. Continue in this way until the end of the round.

Round 3 onwards: Repeat round two until the required length is reached.

Picot Single Crochet

What a super-easy, fun way to add interest to your crochet project! Single picot crochet is yet another variation of a basic crochet stitch with a similar finish to Tunisian crochet. The stitch, designated by the abbreviation "Psc", is ideal for elegant, draped fabric.

For the test sample, make a chain that works in multiples of 2 plus 1. Thus, you can start with 13 chains.

Row 1, First Picot: Insert your hook into the second chain, yarn over, and draw through. Then, into the same chain, repeat the yarn over and pull through three times more. You should have eight loops on your hook. Now, yarn over, and draw the thread through all eight loops. Work one chain to close the picot stitch, which has formed on the RS of the fabric.

Second picot: *Make one single crochet into the next chain, then insert the hook into the following chain stitch, *yarn over, and pull through**. Repeat *...** until there are eight loops on the hook. Yarn over and draw through all eight loops. Work one chain to close the picot stitch**.

Repeat *...** until the end of the row. Turn.

Row 2: Chain one and work a single crochet into every stitch across the row. Turn.

Row 3, First picot: Chain one, then, insert your hook into the second chain, yarn over, and draw through. Into the same chain, yarn over and pull through three times more. You should have eight loops on your hook. Now, yarn over, and draw the thread through all eight loops. Work one chain to close the picot stitch.

Second picot: *Make one single crochet into the next chain, then insert the hook into the following chain stitch, *yarn over, and pull through**. Repeat *...** until there are eight loops on the hook. Yarn over and draw through all eight loops. Work one chain to close the picot stitch**.

Row 4 and every even numbered row: Repeat row two.

Row 5 and every uneven numbered row: Repeat row three.

Continue the repeat the alternate rows until the required project length is reached.

Shell Stitch

Another unique and highly effective crochet stitch, shell stitch, starts with a single crochet foundation. Although the stitch is for advanced beginners, if you are looking for impressive results, why not try the shell stitch?

The shell stitch is very effective with color changes that create a fascinating, intricate design of which you will be proud. You can crochet one row of shells to make an attractive border to almost any fabric, from washcloths, tablecloths, napkins, and hand towels, to throws.

So, if you are ready to learn the shell stitch, grab a hook and suitable yarn, and let's get started. For a stitch sample, work the foundation chain of 19 chains—the shell stitch works in multiples of six plus one.

Row 1: Work a single crochet into the second chain from the hook and into every chain along the row.

Row 2: Start by making one chain and working one single crochet into the same stitch. *Skip one stitch and work five double crochet into the next stitch. Then, skip one stitch and work one single crochet into the following stitch**. Repeat *...** to the end of the row. End with one double crochet.

Row 3: Make three chains and work five double crochet into the next stitch. Now, work one single crochet into the center of the shell in the previous row. *Work five double crochet into the single crochet between the shells in the previous row. Now, work one single crochet into the center of the shell in the previous row**. **Repeat** *...** to the end of the row, finishing with three double crochet in the last single crochet stitch in the previous row.

Repeat rows two and three until the project piece reaches the required length.

Primrose Stitch

The fascinating and easy-to-master primrose stitch is a shell stitch variation. It is worked with double crochet and chain stitches to create a delicate open weave design ideal for washcloths, among other things.

Here are step-by-step instructions, specifically for beginner crocheters.

You will need to work in multiples of three plus 2, so the sampler will start with 14 chain stitches.

Foundation Row: Into the third chain from the hook work (one single crochet, chain two, another single crochet). *Skip two chains and make (one single crochet, chain two, another single crochet)**. Repeat *...** to the row's end. Finish with one half double crochet. Turn.

Row 1: Crochet three chains, * make three dc into the second chain space. Repeat from * to the row's end, finishing with one double crochet worked into the top of the turning chain. Turn your work.

Row 2: Crochet two chains, then work * (one single crochet, two chains, one single crochet) into the second double crochet stitch of the next shell**. Repeat *...** until the end of the row, finishing with one double crochet into the top of the turning chain. Turn your work.

Repeat rows one and two until the required length is reached.

Popcorn Stitch

The popcorn stitch adds dimension, interest, and a touch of glamour to your craft projects and is ideal for growing your crochet collection. Popcorn stitch is a step up from puff and shell stitch, so once you have mastered those two stitches, you are ready to learn the popcorn stitch method, which always uses odd-numbered stitches.

Let's get started on making a sampler. But, first, you'll need yarn and a suitable hook to crochet a foundation chain of nineteen chains.

Row 1: Chain one, and work one single crochet into the second chain and into every chain across the row.

Row 2: Make one chain and *work one single crochet into the first stitch and five double crochet stitches into the next stitch. Then, pull up the last loop of the fifth double crochet to make it longer and remove your hook from the loop. Insert the hook into the first stitch at the top of the double crochet and pick up the long loop, yarn over and draw the thread through the two loops to close the popcorn. Then, work one single crochet into the first stitch after the popcorn, and work five double crochet stitches into the following stitch**. Repeat *...** to the end of the row. Turn.

Row 3: Make one chain and single crochet into every stitch across the back of the row. Note that you should be working into the back loops of the popcorn stitches to make sure these stitches remain puffed out.

Row 4: Make one chain and work one single crochet into the first stitch next to the chain. Then work five double crochet stitches into the next stitch. Pull up the last loop of the fifth double crochet to make it longer, and remove your hook from the loop. Insert the hook into the first stitch at the top of the double crochet and pick up the long loop, yarn over and draw the thread through the two loops to close the popcorn. Then, work one single crochet into the first stitch after the popcorn, and work five double crochet stitches into the following stitch**. Repeat *...** to the end of the row. Turn.

Row 5: Make one chain and single crochet into every stitch across the back of the row. Note that you should be working into the back loops of the popcorn stitches to make sure these stitches remain puffed out.

Repeat rows four and five until the project's required length is reached.

Tips for your success with popcorn stitch:

- The more you work the popcorn stitch, the faster it is likely to go.
- The stitch uses much more yarn than you may expect, so make sure you have enough skeins of the color/colors you plan to use.
- Although popcorn stitch looks similar to bobble stitch, the process is different. So, keep a close watch on your crochet project as you work to make sure you place your hook correctly to get the best stitch results.
- Changing yarn color works in the same way as for shell stitch. Changing the yarn color at the end of the single crochet row works best.
- Well done! You have now mastered another crochet stitch that will add a professional style and glamour to your crafty yarn projects.

CROCHET STITCHES

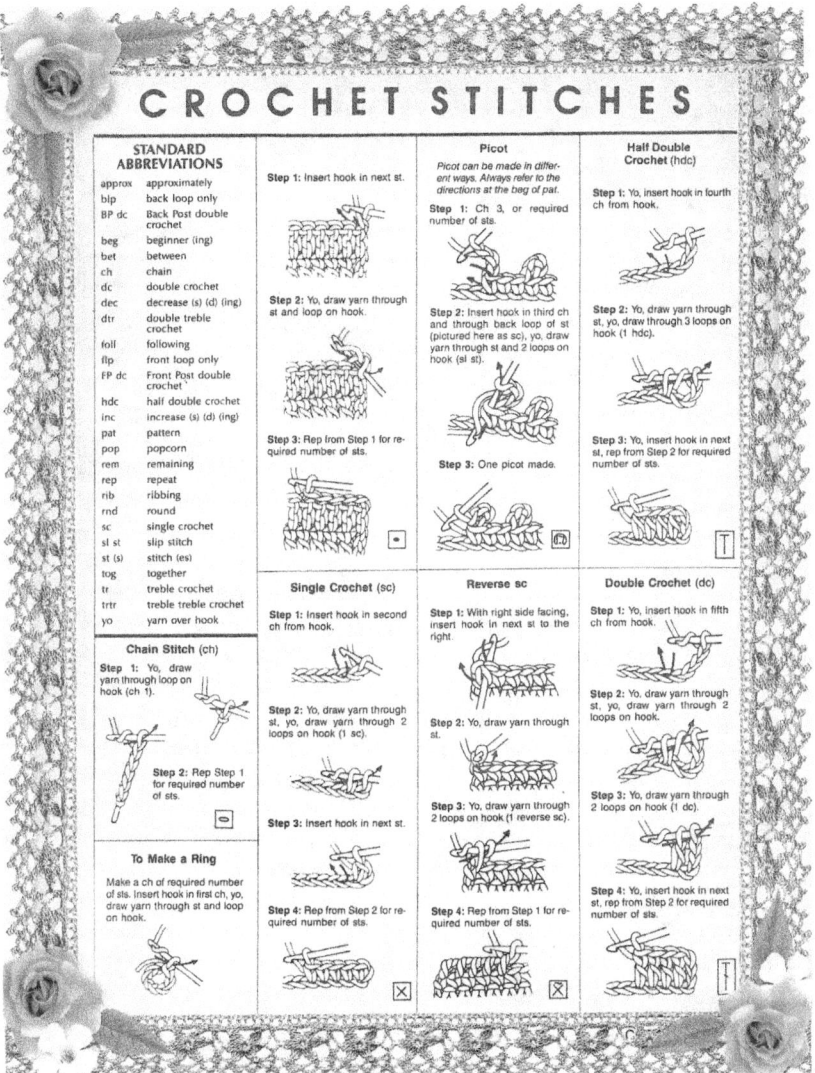

STANDARD ABBREVIATIONS

approx	approximately
blp	back loop only
BP dc	Back Post double crochet
beg	beginner (ing)
bet	between
ch	chain
dc	double crochet
dec	decrease (s) (d) (ing)
dtr	double treble crochet
foll	following
flp	front loop only
FP dc	Front Post double crochet
hdc	half double crochet
inc	increase (s) (d) (ing)
pat	pattern
pop	popcorn
rem	remaining
rep	repeat
rib	ribbing
rnd	round
sc	single crochet
sl st	slip stitch
st (s)	stitch (es)
tog	together
tr	treble crochet
trtr	treble treble crochet
yo	yarn over hook

Chain Stitch (ch)

Step 1: Yo, draw yarn through loop on hook (ch 1).

Step 2: Rep Step 1 for required number of sts.

To Make a Ring

Make a ch of required number of sts. Insert hook in first ch, yo, draw yarn through st and loop on hook.

Step 1: Insert hook in next st.

Step 2: Yo, draw yarn through st and loop on hook.

Step 3: Rep from Step 1 for required number of sts.

Single Crochet (sc)

Step 1: Insert hook in second ch from hook.

Step 2: Yo, draw yarn through st, yo, draw yarn through 2 loops on hook (1 sc).

Step 3: Insert hook in next st.

Step 4: Rep from Step 2 for required number of sts.

Picot

Picot can be made in different ways. Always refer to the directions at the beg of pat.

Step 1: Ch 3, or required number of sts.

Step 2: Insert hook in third ch and through back loop of st (pictured here as sc), yo, draw yarn through st and 2 loops on hook (sl st).

Step 3: One picot made.

Reverse sc

Step 1: With right side facing, insert hook in next st to the right.

Step 2: Yo, draw yarn through st.

Step 3: Yo, draw yarn through 2 loops on hook (1 reverse sc).

Step 4: Rep from Step 1 for required number of sts.

Half Double Crochet (hdc)

Step 1: Yo, insert hook in fourth ch from hook.

Step 2: Yo, draw yarn through st, yo, draw yarn through 3 loops on hook (1 hdc).

Step 3: Yo, insert hook in next st, rep from Step 2 for required number of sts.

Double Crochet (dc)

Step 1: Yo, insert hook in fifth ch from hook.

Step 2: Yo, draw yarn through st, yo, draw yarn through 2 loops on hook.

Step 3: Yo, draw yarn through 2 loops on hook (1 dc).

Step 4: Yo, insert hook in next st, rep from Step 2 for required number of sts.

THE KEY TAKEAWAY

If you are proud of your efforts in learning different crochet stitches, you will want to start crocheting your unique yarn craft project. So, let's find out more about useful crochet apps, plenty of helpful hints for left-handed crocheters, and the answers to some essential questions.

ANSWERING YOUR QUESTIONS

During the Covid pandemic, many people resorted to hobbies and crafts to keep themselves busy and relieve stress. The result has been a crafting boom not seen in many years. Among the most popular arts to grow exponentially, crocheting is one of those handcrafts that has stood the test of time, rallied valiantly, and risen above the mundane to secure a recognized place in the annals of crafting history.

IS IT HARD TO LEARN TO CROCHET?

No, learning to crochet is not hard. However, as with learning any new skill or craft, you must practice and be patient. You may be amazed at how quickly you master holding the hook and yarn to begin doing unique crochet projects.

WHAT'S THE BEST WAY TO LEARN CROCHET?

Depending on your preferences, plenty of books offer super-easy and valuable tips and tricks to learn to crochet. There are tons of internet resources. Also, there are plenty of easily accessible videos detailing step-by-step instructions for every aspect of your crochet journey, from working a foundation chain to crocheting the most intricate stitches. However, sometimes sitting alongside a crochet crafter can make a huge difference in learning the craft. Taking a beginner-friendly course is another option worth considering.

IS IT EASIER TO LEARN CROCHET OR KNITTING?

That depends mainly on the person and their specific projects. Knitting requires both hands to work in unison for a quality finished product. However, crocheting uses one hand only to manipulate the hook and create beautiful, valuable projects. Knitting projects can also take longer to complete than similar crocheted items. Some people find crocheting more fulfilling because achieving specific crochet craft projects takes less time and effort.

Both crafts have pros and cons, so it's up to the individual to choose the craft most comfortable for them.

HOW MANY STITCHES DO I NEED TO LEARN BEFORE STARTING A CROCHET PROJECT?

You can start crocheting many items by learning the four basic stitches: Chain stitch, slip stitch, single crochet, and double crochet.

DO CROCHET PROJECTS USE LESS YARN THAN KNITTED PROJECTS?

Unfortunately not. Crochet projects usually use more yarn than similar knitted projects.

HOW MANY DIFFERENT CROCHET STITCHES ARE THERE?

There may be over a hundred different stitches. However, many of these are variations of the four essential crochet stitches described in Chapter 6.

HOW DO I KEEP TRACK OF STITCHES?

To correctly count stitches, you should know the basics of crochet stitches. As a quick refresher, remember the turning chain sets the stitch height for the remainder of the row. In addition, the turning chain does not usually count as the first stitch in the row.

- Single crochet uses ONE chain.
- Half double crochet uses TWO chains.
- Double crochet uses THREE chains.
- Treble crochet uses FOUR chains.

Counting crochet stitches can be done in two ways:

1. Count by posts. The taller the stitches, the easier they are to count.
2. Count the stitches along the top of the row. The "v's" along the top of a crochet row are easier to count, where each "v" counts as one stitch.

HOW DO I COUNT ROWS?

Remember, the foundation chain does not count as a row.

Using a row counter works well to help you keep track of rows. Otherwise, you can count the stitches along one edge from the bottom to the top of your crochet article to determine the number of rows. For example, if your project is worked in single crochet, each stitch along the edge counts as one row. However, by placing a stitch marker every fifth or tenth row as you work, depending on the size of your project, you will find it easier to count the rows.

HOW DO I CROCHET ROUNDS?

Beginner crocheters prefer to work in rows, as they often find crocheting in rounds somewhat challenging. However, you don't need to feel restricted to working on flat crochet projects. Once you have mastered the basic crochet stitches, you can try your hand at crocheting in rounds. There are plenty of exciting and easy-to-master crochet projects worked in rounds to test your growing crochet skills.

The secret of working rounds is to remember to increase regularly to make sure the circle grows evenly without warping.

There are two ways to crochet rounds.

- One is to work continuously in the round, making a spiral as you crochet. There is no clear start and end point in the round. The spiral method is suitable for coasters, placemats, and some crocheted hats.
- The second way of working rounds is to close each round with a slip stitch. Thus, each round builds on the one before as the height of your project increases. This method is predominantly used on Amigurumi creations and other free-standing, three-dimensional structures.

Either of the working-in-rounds methods is super useful for making coasters to protect your beautiful wood surfaces from wet glasses and coffee mugs.

Let's Start Working a Round Using a Slip Stitch Join

Let's make a magic circle, into which you will work eight chains because you will work half double crochet stitches for the project. See Chapter Five for instructions on making a magic ring. Remember,

- If you have chosen to work single crochet, begin with six stitches.
- Half double crochet should start with eight chains.
- Double crochet will require ten chains.

Round 1: Make two chains and then work seven half double crochet stitches into each of the remaining seven chains in the magic ring. Slip stitch to the top of chain two. The slip stitch counts as one stitch. Pull the yarn tail to close the circle.

Round 2: Make two chains and work one half double crochet into the same stitch as the slip stitch. Work two half double crochets into the next stitch and every other stitch in the round until there are 16 stitches. Slip stitch to the top of chain two. (16 st)

Round 3: Make two chains and work one half double crochet into the same stitch as the slip stitch. Then, work one half double crochet into the next stitch. Now, work *two half double crochet stitches into the following stitch and one half double crochet into the next stitch**. Repeat *...** to the end of the round. Slip stitch into the top of chain two. You should have twenty-four stitches in the round. (24 st)

Round 4: Make two chains and work one half double crochet into the same stitch as the slip stitch. Then, work one half double crochet into each of the next two stitches. Now, *work two half double crochet into the next stitch and one half double crochet stitch into each of the following two stitches**. Repeat *...** to the end of the round. You should have thirty-two stitches. (32 st)

Round 5: Make two chains and work one half double crochet into the same stitch as the slip stitch. Then, work one half double crochet into the following three stitches. Now, *work two half double crochet into the next stitch and one half double crochet into each of the following three stitches**. Repeat *...** to the end of the round. You should have forty stitches in total. (40 st)

Round 6: Make two chains and work one half double crochet into the slip stitch. Then, work one half double crochet into the following four stitches. Now, *work two half double crochet into the next stitch and then work one half double into the following four stitches**. Repeat *...** to the end of the round. Slip stitch into the top of chain two. (48 st)

Round 7: Make two chains and work one half double into each of the next five stitches. Now, *work two half double crochet into the next stitch and one half double crochet into each of the following five stitches**. **Repeat** *...*** until the end of the round. Slip stitch to the top of the second chain. (56 st)

You will notice how much easier it is to see and count each round when you use a slip stitch to close each round.

Let's Try Working Continuous Rounds

First, decide on the crochet stitch you want to use for your unique project. Your choice will dictate the number of stitches you need to start.

- If you have chosen to work single crochet, begin with six stitches.
- Half double crochet should start with eight chains.
- Double crochet will require ten chains.

For example, let's make a magic circle into which you will work eight chains because you will work half double crochet stitches for the project. See Chapter Five for instructions for crocheting a magic ring.

Round 1: Make two chains and work seven half double crochet stitches into the magic circle. You should have eight stitches. (8 st)

Round 2: Work one half double crochet into the next stitch. Mark this first stitch using a stitch marker. Now, work a second half double crochet into the same stitch. Then work two half double crochet stitches into every stitch along the round. (16 st)

Round 3: Remove the stitch marker. Work one half double crochet into that stitch and replace the marker in the stitch you have just worked. Work a second half double crochet into the same stitch. Then, work one half double crochet into the next stitch. Now, *work two half double crochet into the next stitch and one half double into the following stitch**. Repeat *...** to the end of the round. (24 st)

Round 4: Remove the stitch marker. Work one half double crochet into that stitch and replace the marker in the stitch you have just worked. Work a second half double crochet into the same stitch. Then, work one half double crochet into the next three stitches. Now, *work two half double crochet stitches into the next and one half double crochet into the following two stitches**. Repeat *...** to the end of the round. (32 st)

Round 5: Remove the stitch marker. Work one half double crochet into that stitch and replace the marker in the stitch you have just worked. Work a second half double crochet into the same stitch. Then, work one half double crochet into the next three stitches. Now, *work two half double crochet stitches into the next stitch and one half double crochet into the following three stitches**. Repeat *...** to the end of the round. (40 st)

Round 6: Remove the stitch marker. Work one half double crochet into that stitch and replace the marker in the stitch you have just worked. Work a second half double crochet into the same stitch. Then, work one half double crochet into the following four stitches. Now, *work two half double crochet stitches into the next stitch and one half double crochet into the following four stitches**. **Repeat** *...** to the end of the round. (48 st)

You will see that the pattern developing resembles a spiral, making the rounds challenging to count without stitch markers in place.

HOW DO I COUNT ROUNDS?

The easiest way to count rounds is to use a stitch counter that doubles for tallying rows and rounds. However, you can mark rounds using stitch/row markers. As you complete each round add a stitch marker. Once you have five stitch markers, leave the fifth marker in place and remove the markers below. Eventually, depending on the project's height, every fifth round will carry a stitch marker, so it's easy to count the number of rounds.

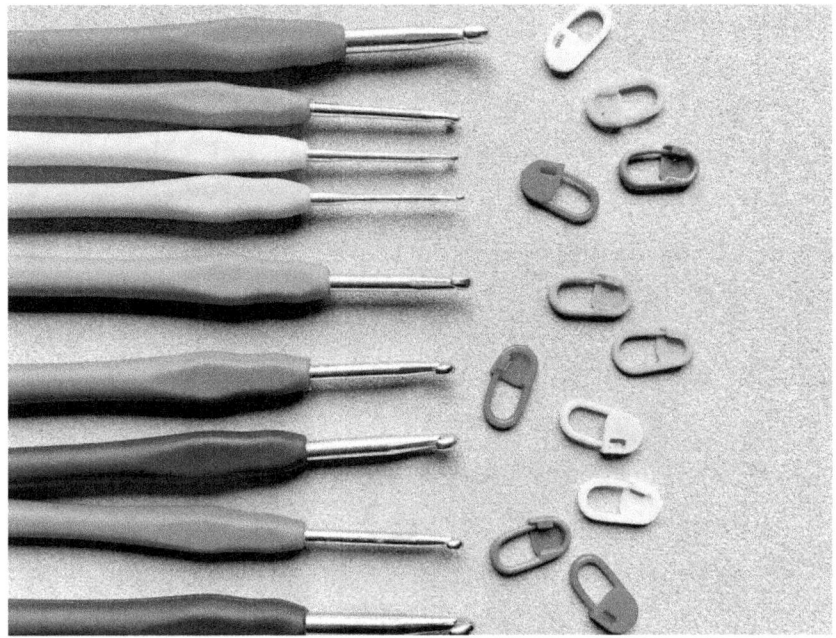

HOW DO I KEEP YARN TENSION?

Your crochet project's success depends heavily on yarn tension. Many beginner crocheters find achieving the correct tension isn't as easy as it sounds. First, you should make sure your hook grip in your preferred hand is comfortable and not strained.

Here are several more helpful tips to help you master the technique of keeping tension correct.

Yarn From the Skein's Center

Pull yarn from the middle of the skein to avoid yarn snags. The yarn unravels quickly and is likely to run smoothly through your fingers, ensuring the tension is even.

Tension Regulator

You may find wearing a finger regulator on your index finger, through which the yarn runs, will help regulate tension. You can weave a small yarn regulating ring or purchase one online or from your local craft store.

To make your neat, functional tension regulator ring, use worsted weight yarn and a 4 mm hook.

- Work nine chains and join the last chain to the first using a slip stitch, to create a ring.
- Work three chains, then make one double crochet into each chain around the ring. Join with a slip stitch to the top of chain three.
- Make three chains and work the second round of double crochet into each stitch. Be sure to insert your hook under the "v" stitches in the previous round. Join with a slip stitch to the top of chain three.
- Make three chains and work the third round of double crochet into each stitch. Be sure to insert your hook under the "v" stitches in the previous round. Join with a slip stitch to the top of chain three. Fasten off the yarn and weave the end neatly into the ring.
- Place the tension regulator ring on the index finger of your yarn hand.

- Insert the hook between two double crochet stitches. Pull your working yarn end through the regulator ring and make the slip knot to start the required foundation chain. The yarn pulls through the regulator as you work, keeping the tension even.

HOW DO I CREATE AN EVEN EDGE?

You will agree that uneven edges spoil the best crochet projects, but creating even edges takes a little extra time and focus.

Essential tips to bear in mind.

- Be sure you insert your hook into the first and last stitch of every row.
- Choosing to turn your work clockwise or counterclockwise is usually a significant personal choice. Whichever way you choose, be consistent to create an even edge.
- Check that every row starts with the correct turning chain. See Chapter Six for the number of chains you need for the different stitches. For example, when you work double crochet, always start with three chains in the turning chain at the beginning of each double crochet row. End each row with a double crochet into the top of the turning chain in the previous row.

- Sometimes, the last stitch ends up as the second to the last stitch in a row. Crochet into every stitch on the previous row to avoid the gap forming. So, if there are seventeen stitches in the previous row, make sure you work the same number of stitches in every row to maintain an even edge.
- You may want to start every row with single crochet. Then work another single crochet into the first single crochet. Now, continue with double crochet across the row. The single crochet stitches stack neatly to make an attractive, neat, and even edge.
- Keep counting the stitches in each row. Having too many or too few stitches will create uneven edges.
- And finally, edging your flat project with a row of single crochet will make all the difference in creating a neat, even edge.

HOW DO I JOIN YARN COLORS?

Many exciting and attractive crochet designs require a yarn color change. Always reserve these color changes for the ends of rows where the yarn tail can hang without complicating your crocheting process, and each new row starts in a different color.

Whether changing the yarn color at the end of a row or joining a new ball of yarn mid-row, the instructions apply to both scenarios. Work the new color or renewed yarn in the same way, as detailed below.

- Work along a row until two loops of the last stitch in the row remain on your hook. Yarn over with the new color and pull the thread through the two loops on the hook to complete the stitch.
- Turn your work, making the required number of chains to suit the crochet stitch you are using for the project. Continue following the stitches and pattern instructions.
- If you plan the color change every alternate row, do not snip the yarn with which you finish the row. Simply carry a loose loop of the yarn up to the following row when you need it again.
- However, if there are more than four rows between color changes, snip the yarn, leaving a tail of about 2-3 inches (5-7 cm).
- When the color change comes in the middle of a row, work the last stitch before changing to the last two loops on the hook before, working in the new color.

VALUABLE TIPS FOR LEFT-HANDED BEGINNER CROCHETERS

Most left-handed crocheters who started the yarn craft years ago were forced to learn to reverse crochet from their right-handed co-crafters. Fortunately, there is now a great deal of information specific to left-handed crocheters, including patterns, books, and helpful videos to assist in mastering natural left-handed skills.

How Do I Hold the Hook?

As Chapter Five discusses, learning to grasp your hook and yarn is no more challenging than for right-handed crochet crafters. Finding the most comfortable grip is the best solution. So, practice the pencil and knife grips to find the best fit for your unique style.

Are There Crochet Patterns for Left-handed Crocheters?

Most crochet patterns, symbol charts, and tutorials are prepared for right-handed crocheters. However, if you are left-handed, follow the crochet instructions, charts, and patterns in the opposite direction. Therefore, you will work your first row into the foundation chain from left to right. And, when you work crochet rounds, you will work clockwise. As you work, your crochet direction must allow you a clear view of your stitches.

How Do I Make a Foundation Chain?

Make a slip knot on your hook, as explained in Chapter Five. Yarn over and scoop the thread clockwise through the loop. Yarn over again and pull through another chain. Each repetition makes one chain. Continue until you have the required number of chains for your project.

How Do I Single Crochet?

Once the foundation chain has reached the required number of chains, working left to right, insert your hook into the second chain from your hook. *Yarn over clockwise. Draw up a loop. You will notice that there are two loops on your hook. Yarn over again and pull the thread through both loops**.

Insert the hook into the next chain and repeat from *...** to complete the second single crochet. Repeat the process until you reach the end of the first row.

Then, make one chain and turn your work in preparation for working the second row.

Will I Manage Double Crochet?

Most left-handed crocheters cope just fine with double crochet. Once you have mastered the fluid movements for single crochet, the only difference in double crochet is an extra step.

Working left to right, yarn clockwise over your hook. Insert the hook into the fourth chain from the hook and yarn over. Pull up the thread. You should have three loops on your hook.

Yarn over and pull the thread through two loops. Then, yarn over again and pull the thread through the remaining two loops. You have completed the first double crochet.

*Yarn over, insert your hook into the next chain. Pull up a loop. Yarn over again and pull the thread through two loops. Repeat yarn over and pull the thread through the last two loops**.

Repeat *...** until you reach the end of the row. You have completed your first row of double crochet!

Make three chains and turn your work in preparation for the second double crochet row.

Is Treble Crochet Difficult for Left-handed Crocheters?

Learning treble crochet is no more challenging than double crochet. Once you have mastered the crocheting technique, you will find it easier to make new stitches.

Treble crochet is similar to double crochet except for one extra step. So, let's begin.

▷ First Treble Crochet Stitch

- Working left to right on your foundation chain, yarn twice over the hook. Insert your hook into the fifth stitch from your hook and pull up a loop. There should be four loops on your hook, which will form the first treble.
- Yarn over again and draw the thread through two loops.
- Yarn over again and draw the thread through another two loops.
- Yarn over for the last time, and draw the thread through the final two loops, leaving one loop on your hook.

▷ Second Treble Crochet Stitch

- Now, for the second treble crochet stitch, *wrap the yarn three times over your hook and insert the hook into the next stitch. Yarn over again. There should be four loops on the hook.
- Yarn over again. Draw the yarn through two loops. There should be three loops remaining on the hook.
- Yarn over again. Draw the yarn through two loops. There should now be two loops.
- Yarn over once again. Draw the yarn through the two loops, leaving one loop on the hook**.

- Repeat from * to ** to complete the first row of treble crochet.

USEFUL CROCHET APPS

For those crafty crocheters who enjoy innovative opportunities to discover new and exciting ways of learning crochet skills online, there are plenty of exciting teaching apps suitable for your iPod, iPhone, iPad, or laptop. Here are a few apps to whet your interest.

Graphghan Creator

This super-useful app offers crafters, especially crocheters, an innovative pattern creator for your mobile device. The Graphghan Creator app may be helpful to left-handed crocheters who want to reverse right-handed patterns for easier working.

Quick and Easy Crochet Magazine

This online magazine features up-to-date crochet hints, fashions, and ideas for any crafters interested in improving their creative crochet skills.

All Free Crochet

This app, updated daily, is ideal for beginner crocheters interested in learning more crochet skills. *All Free Crochet* offers a selection of funky, trendy, and valuable free crochet patterns and tutorials.

Crochet!

The online crochet magazine "Crochet!" is packed with stunning crochet designs and ideas. There are heaps of pieces of helpful advice for beginner crocheters who enjoy surfing the web for new ideas.

A Needle Pulling Thread

This interesting app offers an exciting and informative craft magazine that provides plenty of valuable hints and tips for various crafts, including crochet.

PatternCraft App

The PatternCraft App offers many exciting ideas for crocheters and other crafters to develop their unique designs and patterns for specific craft projects.

Simple Crochet

This app offers various innovative designs and gorgeous ideas for crafty crocheters. The easy-to-follow instructions make online learning a new and accessible technique for many avid yarn crafters with a passion for crochet.

Crochet Facebook Groups

You can find plenty of helpful hints and support for all your crochet projects from like-minded, enthusiastic yarn crafters who share their ideas in Facebook crochet groups worldwide.

THE KEY TAKEAWAY

Wow! There is an abundance of helpful information for beginner crocheters in the previous chapters. All in all, you should have mastered the basic crochet stitches, and you are probably brimming with enthusiasm to start a crochet project. So, grab your hook, yarn, and crochet kit, and let's get started making something you can use, wear or display with pride.

OBTAINING FREE PATTERNS

Many beginner crocheters may wonder where they can source the best patterns for their new and exciting crochet projects. As many designs can be expensive, there are plenty of online sources for suitable free patterns.

FUNCTIONAL WEAR

Here are several easy-to-crochet patterns, ideal for beginner crocheters and anyone looking to brush up on their yarn craft skills.

Quick and Easy Heelless Socks

Ideal for beginner crocheters, you can create these socks in an evening. The fun thing about the pattern is that you can crochet the socks to fit almost any size by working extra rows.

This pair of socks fit a medium-sized foot measuring about 6-8 inches (15-20 cm).

Materials—worsted weight yarn, #4 in the color of your choice, hook size: I-9 (5.5 mm). Alternatively, you can use cotton and an H hook.

Instructions

Make two identical socks.

Make a slip knot and work six chains.

Round 1: Work one "sc" into the second chain from your hook. Work four "sc" along the row into the last chain. Now, work "sc" into the lower edge of each chain until you reach the start of the round. Slip stitch into the first chain.

Round 2: Chain one and work two "sc" into the next stitch. Then work "sc" into each of the next five stitches. Work two "sc" into each of the following two stitches. Now, work "sc" into each of the next six stitches. Slip stitch into the first chain of the round.

Round 3: Chain one, work two sc into the next two stitches and one "sc" into the following six stitches. Work two "sc" into each of the next two stitches and one "sc" into the following eight stitches. Slip stitch to close the round.

Round 4: Chain one, work two "sc" into the next two stitches. Work one "sc" into the following nine stitches. Work two "sc" into the next two stitches, and one "sc" into the next ten stitches. Slip stitch to close the round.

Round 5: Chain two, work one "hdc" into each stitch to the end of the round. Slip stitch to close the round. The sock toe is now complete. (30 st)

Round 6: Chain three and work one "dc" into each stitch over the round. Slip stitch to close the round.

Round 7: Chain three and decrease by working one "dc" into the next two stitches together. Work one "dc" into the next 13 stitches. Then decrease by working one "dc" into the following two stitches. Now, work one "dc" into the next 13 stitches and slip stitch into the third chain.

Rounds 8: Chain two and work one "hdc" into every stitch over the round. Slip stitch to close the round.

Round 9: Repeat round eight.

Rounds 10-12: Chain one, work one "sc" into each stitch over the round. Slip stitch into the top of the starting chain.

Round 13: Chain three, work one "dc" into every stitch across the round. Slip stitch into the top chain of the starting chain.

Rounds 14-16: Repeat round 13.

Rounds 16-19: Repeat round eight.

Rounds 20-24: Repeat round thirteen until you reach the required length.

Finishing off: Work two rounds of "sc" into each stitch to give a neat sock edge.

Fingerless Mittens

Fashionable fingerless mittens make a delightful and easy-to-crochet project for beginner yarn crafters. Adjust the mitten length and width to fit individual wearers.

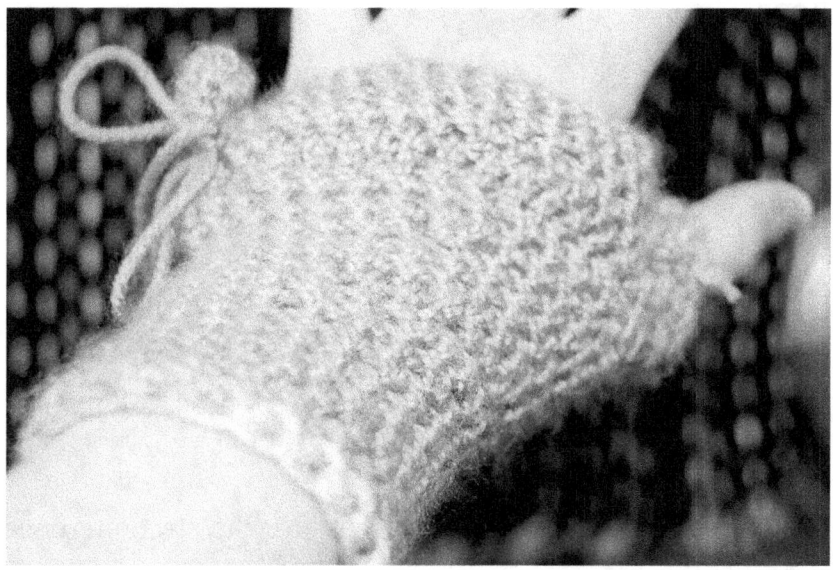

Materials—five ounces of worsted weight yarn #4, hook size: G6 (4.5 mm). You can use cotton and an H hook.

Instructions

Make two identical rectangles. Make sure you make a left and right mitten when you seam the edges.

Crochet a foundation of 30 chains.

Row 1: Chain one, and work one "sc" into the second chain from your hook and into every chain until the end of the row. There should be 30 stitches in the first row. Turn your work and make one chain.

Row 2: Chain two and work one "hdc" into each stitch across the row.

Row 3: Repeat row two.

Row 4: Chain one and work one "sc" into each stitch across the row.

Rows 5 and 6: Repeat row four.

Rows 7 and 8: Repeat two.

Continue alternating two rows of "sc" with two rows of "hdc" until the project reaches the desired size. You may need to add rows for larger dimensions.

To determine the mitten's size, measure the circumference around the widest part of the hand of the person for whom you are doing the project. Make sure to check the mitten length before finishing the final row. Leave a yarn tail of about 20 inches. Fold each of the mittens with the right side inside. Whipstitch the seam from right to left, leaving a gap of about two to three inches for the thumb. Fasten off the yarn with a secure, neat knot or back stitch. Thread the yarn tail neatly into the seam. Sew an attractive button to the top of each mitten.

Beanie in a Jiffy

Another easy-to-crochet beginner's project is this quick, warm beanie.

Materials—any worsted weight, acrylic #3 yarn, hook size: G6 (4 mm)

The finished beanie measures about 10 inches, with a circumference of 22 inches. You can adjust the measurements to fit any size head.

Gauge—eight double crochet in four inches. Change the hook size to decrease/increase the gauge.

Instructions

Make a foundation chain with 80 chains.

Row 1: Chain one and work one "sc" into every chain across the row. Turn.

Row 2 and 3: Chain two and work one "hdc" into every stitch across the row. Turn.

Row 4 and 5: Chain three and work one "dc" into every stitch across the row.

Alternate "hdc" and "dc" rows until you reach nine inches. Adjust the length to the person's head.

Secure the short edges with stitch markers to keep them from slipping. Working on the WS, slip stitch the seam to form a tube. Finish with a secure back stitch or a neat knot.

Do not cut the yarn tail. Instead, thread the yarn tail through the top stitches of the tube. Pull the thread to gather the fabric top. Secure the yarn with a neat knot and incorporate the yarn tail into the seam. Trim off excess yarn ends.

Turn the beanie RS out. Add a pompom or similar embellishment to the top of the beanie.

Baby Booties

These booties are perfect for keeping tiny feet cozy.

Materials—worsted weight, baby yarn #3, hook size G6 (4 mm).

Instructions

Make two similar booties.

Make 53 chains.

Row 1: Work one "hdc" into the second chain from the hook and into every chain until the end. Turn and chain two.

Row 2: Work one "hdc" into each stitch of the row.

Repeat row two until the work measures 2 inches (5 cm).

Then, chain two, work one "hdc" into each of the 17 stitches. Decrease by working one "hdc" into the following two stitches six times. Then, work one "hdc" into the next stitch. Again, decrease by working one "hdc" into the following two stitches six times. Now, work one "hdc" into 17 stitches. End the row with one "hdc". Turn your work.

Now, chain three and work one "dc" into each of the 17 stitches on the left side of the bootie. Turn, chain three, and work one "dc" into each of the same 17 stitches. Finally, snip the yarn, leaving a two-inch tail. Pull the tail through the last loop on your hook and finish the row with a neat knot.

Rejoin the yarn at the straight edge on the right side of the bootie. Now, chain three and work one "dc" into each of the 17 stitches on the right side of the bootie. Next, turn, chain three, and work one "dc" into each of the same 17 stitches. Finally, snip the yarn, leaving a two-inch tail. Pull the tail through the last loop on your hook and finish the row with a neat knot.

Turn the bootie RS in and whipstitch the seam from the outer corners to the center of the sole. Then, turn the bootie RS out.

Bootie ties (make four)—Work 16 chains. Turn, make one "sc" into the second chain from the hook. Work "sc" into every chain until the end of the row. Fasten off the yarn leaving a three-inch tail. Using a yarn needle, attach the ties to each bootie's left and right raised corners.

FASHION ACCESSORIES

Crochet accessories have become the trendy go-to style for adding glitz and glamor to everyday wear.

Trendy Headband

Keep your ears warm during the cold weather by working a beautiful headband out of yarn scraps. The band fits an average adult woman.

Materials—worsted weight, medium #4 or chunky #5 yarn, hook size: I9 (5.5 mm) / L (7 mm)

Instructions

Make 60 chains.

Row 1: Chain one and work one "sc" into the second chain from the hook. Then, work one "sc" into every stitch until the end of the row. Turn and chain three.

Row 2: Chain two and work one "hdc" into every stitch along the row.

Row 3: Chain three and work one "dc" into every stitch across the row.

Rows 4 and 5: Repeat row three.

Row 6: Repeat row two.

Row 7: Repeat row one.

Check the bandwidth and add more rows (row 3) if needed.

Fasten off the yarn, leaving about a 10-inch tail.

Using the yarn tail, slipstitch the straight edges together. Fasten the yarn off securely and thread the tail into the seam.

The trendy crocheted headband lends an elegant, fashionable touch to complement a suitable ensemble.

Boho Belt

Materials—use two colors of 100% cotton yarn, best suited to a size H8 (5 mm).

Instructions

Work in multiples of two. The number of chains will determine how long the belt will be.

Using the first color, for example, white, chain up about five feet, and turn.

Row 1: Work two "dc" into the fourth chain from the hook. Skip one chain and work two "dc" into the following chain. Continue in the same way until the end of the row. If you want to change the yarn color, leave the last two loops of the last "dc" on the hook. Pull the new color, for example, teal, through and chain three. Turn.

Row 2: Skip one space and work two "dc" into the center "v" of the two "dc" in the previous row. *Skip one space and work two "dc" into the next "v" between the two "dc" in the previous row**. Repeat *...** until the end of the row—chain three and turn.

Row 3: Repeat row two using the teal yarn. If you want to change yarn color, for example, back to the white thread, leave two loops of the last stitch on the hook. Pull up a loop of the white yarn, secure the loop, and chain three. Turn.

Row 4: Repeat row three to the end of the row. Fasten off the yarn. Thread the tail neatly into the edge of the belt.

Well done! You have just completed your first crochet belt.

Stylish Scarf

The scarf is an ideal beginner crochet project. Depending on your unique style, you can use a single color or multiple colors.

Materials—worsted weight yarn #4 or #5, depending on the thickness of the scarf you like to wear. Hook size I9 (5.5 mm) or L (7 mm).

Instructions

Make a foundation chain of 25 chains.

Row 1: Work one "tr" into the fourth chain from the hook and into every chain along the row. Turn.

Row 2: Chain four. Work one "tr" in each chain space in the row. Turn.

Row 3: Repeat row two until the required scarf length is reached.

Tip: You can change the color on each or every alternate row.

Fasten off and weave the yarn tail into the scarf edge.

UNIQUE HOUSEHOLD ITEMS

There are plenty of beautiful, practical projects you can design and crochet for your home. Let's start with the simple coaster to protect your wood table from water marks and stains.

Coasters

You can use a variety of yarn scraps for this project. Cotton yarn works well, with hook size H8 (5 mm).

Instructions

Make a magic circle.

Round 1: Make two chains and work seven "hdc" stitches into the magic circle. You should have eight stitches. (8 st)

Round 2: Work one "hdc" into the next stitch. Mark this first stitch using a stitch marker. Now, work a second "hdc" into the same stitch. Then, work two "hdc" stitches into every stitch around. (16 st)

Round 3: Remove the stitch marker. Work one "hdc" into that stitch and replace the marker in the stitch you have just worked. Work a second "hdc" into the same stitch. Then, work one "hdc" into the next stitch. Now, *work two "hdc" into the next stitch and one "hdc" into the following stitch**. Repeat *...** to the end of the round. (24 st)

Fasten off the yarn. Thread the tail neatly into the coaster's edge.

You may want to crochet a decorative edge around each coaster for added color, fascination, and glamor.

Washcloth

Washcloths have many uses. They can be crocheted from yarn scraps and worked up in an evening.

Materials—100% cotton yarn works best as it is highly absorbent. Hook size G6-H8 (4-5 mm)

Instructions

Make a foundation chain with thirty-one chains.

Row 1: Work one "sc" into the second stitch from your hook and into every stitch along the row. Turn.

Row 2: Chain one, work one "sc" for each stitch along the row. Turn.

Row 3 onwards: Repeat with the second row until the washcloth is the right size. Fasten off the yarn and thread the yarn tail neatly into the washcloth's edge.

TOYS AND OTHER ITEMS

If you are excited to try crochet toys, here are some that are easy to crochet.

Amigurumi Mini Ladybug

The cute ladybug makes an ideal stocking stuffer or child's gift.

Materials—cotton, DK yarn, two 8 mm safety eyes, several black sequins, hook size C (3 mm), stitch markers, non-toxic toy stuffing.

Instructions

Using black yarn, make a magic ring.

Round 1: Crochet six "dc" into the magic ring and join with a slip stitch.

Round 2: Work two "dc" into every stitch in the round. (12 st)

Round 3: Work two "dc" into the first stitch and one "dc" into the next stitch. Then, *work two "dc" into the following stitch and one "dc" into the next stitch**. Repeat *...** round. (18 st)

Round 4: Repeat row three.

Round 5: Repeat row three.

Attach the safety eyes and check the eye placement before securing the safety disk.

Change the yarn color and work seven rounds in red. (18 st)

Round 13: Work 11 decreases: pick up the first two stitch-loops, yarn over, and pull the thread through all three loops. Then, pick up the next two stitch loops and repeat the decrease nine more times.

Now, pull the working loop up a little so as not to lose the stitch. Remove your hook. Stuff the ladybug. Then, insert your hook back into the loop, tighten the loop and work the final two decreases.

Using the yarn tail, close the hole securely. Fasten off the yarn and thread the yarn tail into the ladybug.

Using black yarn, stitch two long threads from the center of the head down the back to demarcate the wings. Then, sew three to four sequins into each wing. You may prefer to embroider yarn spots in place of sequins.

Granny Square Tote

The project is perfect for using yarn scraps to make a colorful tote.

Materials—DK acrylic yarn scrap and appropriate size hooks, I9-J10 (5.5-6 mm). Check the label for hook size and care instructions if you buy yarn.

Instructions

Make eight granny squares as per the pattern below.

Crochet six chains. Insert your hook into the first chain, yarn over, and pull the thread through the two loops on your hook.

Row 1: Chain three to make the first "leg" of the "dc". Yarn over, insert the hook into the middle of the ring, yarn over, and pull up a loop. There should be three loops on your hook. Yarn over, pull the thread through two loops, yarn over again, and pull the thread through two loops again. You have made the second "dc". Remember that three chains act as the first "dc".

Now, yarn over, insert the hook into the middle of the ring, yarn over, and pull up a loop. There should be three loops on your hook. Yarn over, pull the thread through two loops, yarn over again, and pull the thread through two loops again. You have completed the third "dc" in the first cluster.

Now, chain three for the first corner. Then, *yarn over and insert the hook into the middle of the ring, yarn over, and pull up a loop. There should be three loops on your hook. Yarn over, pull the thread through two loops, yarn over again, and pull the thread through two loops again**. Repeat *...** twice more. You have completed the second cluster.

Chain three for the second corner. Then, *yarn over, insert the hook into the middle of the ring, yarn over, and pull up a loop. There should be three loops on your hook. Yarn over, pull the thread through two loops, yarn over again, and pull the thread through two loops again**. Repeat *...** twice more. You have completed the third cluster.

Now, chain three for the third corner. Then, *yarn over, insert the hook into the middle of the ring, yarn over, and pull up a loop. There should be three loops on your hook. Yarn over, pull the thread through two loops, yarn over again, and pull the thread through two loops again**. Repeat *...** twice more. You have completed the fourth cluster.

Chain three and insert the hook into the third chain to complete the fourth corner.

Row 2: Chain four, and work three "dc" into the first corner. Chain three and work another three "dc" into the same corner.

Now, chain three, work three "dc" into the second corner, chain three, and crochet three "dc" into the same corner.

Then, chain three, work three "dc" into the third corner, chain three, and crochet three "dc" into the same corner.

Now, chain three, work three "dc" into the fourth corner, chain three, and work two "dc" into the same corner. To finish the last "dc" cluster, insert your hook into the third chain to complete the last "dc" cluster.

Notice there are two "dc" clusters in each corner.

Row 3: Chain four, work two "dc" into the first space, chain one and work three "dc" into the first corner, chain three and work three "dc" into the same corner.

Then, chain one and work three "dc" into the second corner, chain three and work three "dc" into the same corner.

Now, chain one, work three "dc" into the third corner, chain three, and crochet three "dc" into the same corner.

Then, chain one, work three "dc" into the fourth corner, and chain three and work three "dc" into the same corner. Now, chain one and insert your hook into the third chain to complete the row.

Row 4: Chain four, work three "dc" into the first space, chain one, work three "dc" into the next space, chain one and work three "dc" into the first corner, chain three, work three "dc" into the same corner.

Now, chain one, work three "dc" into the first space, chain one, work three "dc" into the second space, chain one and work three "dc" into the second corner, chain three, work three "dc" into the same corner.

Bag Handle

You can adjust the handle length for personal preference.

Crochet 35 chains.

Row 1: Work one "sc" into the second chain from the hook. Work one "sc" into every chain across the row. Turn.

Row 2: Chain two, work one "sc" on each stitch in each row. Turn.

Row 3-5: Repeat row two.

Fasten off the yarn and thread the yarn tail neatly into the handle's edge.

Assembling the Bag

Seam four granny squares together to make two larger squares.

Orient the two large squares RS towards each other and sew three edges. Turn the bag RS out. Attach the handle from the top edge of one side seam to the other.

THE KEY TAKEAWAY

Great job! You have completed several exciting crochet projects. Now you can allow your natural creativity to blossom as you grow your crochet skills to create an endless variety of beautiful items.

CONCLUSION

This once-unfamiliar yarn craft of crocheting has opened new opportunities to showcase your creative skills. Crocheting is not only a relaxing hobby, it is an art that supports unique innovative artistic expression for young and old. In addition, the yarn craft has sharpened your vibrant interest in handmade projects and whetted your creative appetite.

You have mastered basic crochet stitches and expanded your skills to encompass several new designs. The excitement and pleasure of crafting distinctive crochet projects are hard to beat. You can read a crochet pattern and understand the once-foreign symbols, and your interest in more adventuresome projects has been piqued.

Your knowledge of yarn types and weights has made it easier to choose the best yarn for your ingenious crochet designs. In addition, the easy accessibility to helpful hints and valuable yarn crafting information is right here at your fingertips.

Now that you have a solid crocheting foundation, you can design and make many beautiful things for your home, family, and friends. So, gather up your tools and get hooked on crocheting!

WHAT ARE YOUR THOUGHTS?

Are you enjoying the book?
Have you learned something new?
Has it helped you improve your crochet skills?
Will you recommend it to others?

Let me and your fellow crocheters know by leaving your review on Amazon!
Here's how: just log into your Amazon Account and hit "Orders," click on this book and choose "Leave a Review."

Alternatively, you can scan the QR code below or visit the link to Leave a Review:

https://www.amazon.com/review/create-review/?asin=
B0BDXK94N2

By leaving your review, you are helping to make this book successful, and by doing that, helping others learn and improve their crochet skills and creativity!

Thank you very much

-Genevieve

GLOSSARY

Abbreviations: Contracted or short forms standing for the original word.

Alpaca yarn: Yarn made from the wool of the South American llama.

Amigurumi: Tiny crocheted toys that originated in Japan.

Angora: Yarn made from the hair of the Angora rabbit or goat.

Bohemian: Non-conformist, artsy person.

Cashmere: Soft, fine wool from the Kashmir goat.

Chenille: A velvety yarn or cord.

Cloche hat: A bell-shaped hat, usually worn by women.

Croc: Hook (German).

Croche: Hook (French).

Crochet: The art of crafting yarn using a hook.

Decrease: Reduce the number of stitches.

Ergonomic: Allowing people and things to interact most efficiently and safely.

Etsy: An e-commerce site for buying and selling goods.

Feng Shui: Chinese practice governing the spatial arrangement of furniture, plants, and objects to facilitate improved energy flow (chi).

Filigree: Fine, ornamental lattice work.

Foundation chain: Series of chain stitches, starting with a slip knot that creates the starting row for many crochet projects.

Gauge: Size.

Haken: Crocheting (Netherlands).

Haekling: Crocheting (Denmark).

Hekling: Crocheting (Norway).

Hypoallergenic: Unlikely to cause an allergic reaction.

Increase: Augment the number of stitches.

Insomnia: The inability to easily fall asleep and stay asleep.

Macramé: Knotted rope or cord craft.

Magic circle: Starting a crochet project with an adjustable ring for working in rounds.

Merino: A wool type from sheep of the same name.

Motif: A decorative repeated design forming a pattern.

Plies: The number of yarn strands.

Slip knot: Starting, adjustable knot for crochet/knitting projects.

Slip stitch: Slipping one stitch through another to make an invisible join.

Stitch markers: Small plastic or metal gadgets to hook into crochet fabric to help you keep track of stitch, row, and round numbers.

Symbols: Marks or characters representing specific terms or instructions.

Tambouring: The crochet art of pushing thread through fabric stretched over a frame.

Turning chain: The chain used to start a new row.

Yarn over: Wrapping yarn around the crochet hook to make a new stitch.

Virkning: Crocheting (Sweden).

Worsted weight: Medium-weight yarn.

REFERENCES

All Free Crochet. (2022). *Pineapple stitch.* Allfreecrochet. https://www. allfreecrochet.com/tag/Pineapple-stitch

Murray, A. (2019, Aug. 21). *"V" double crochet tutorial.* Dream a little bigger. https://www.dreamalittlebigger.com/post/v-double-crochet-stitch.html

Brittain, S., & Manthey, K. (2017, April 12). *How to yarn over in crochet.* Dummies. https://www.dummies.com/article/home-auto-hobbies/crafts/ knitting-crocheting/how-to-yarn-over-in-crochet-197672/

Craft Yarn Council. (2021). *Crochet abbreviations.* Www.craftyarncouncil.com. https://www.craftyarncouncil.com/standards/crochet-abbreviations

Crafting in the Night. (2022). *Best crochet hooks for carpal tunnel.* Crafting in the Night. https://craftinginthenight.com/best-crochet-hooks-for-carpal-tunnel/

Crafting in the Night. (2022). *How do you keep the yarn tension when crocheting.* Crafting in the Night. https://craftinginthenight.com/how-do-you-keep-the-yarn-tension-when-crocheting/

Crafty with ashy. (2022). *Is crocheting a good hobby?* Crafty with Ashy. https:// craftywithashy.com/is-crocheting-a-good-hobby-is-it-worth-it/

Crochetbug. (2022). *How to make your own crochet tension regulator.* Crochet-bug. https://crochetbug.com/free-crochet-patterns/how-to-make-your-own-crochet-tension-regulator/

Davina. (2019, May 28). *What is worsted weight yarn? the ultimate beginner's guide.* Sheep and Stitch. https://sheepandstitch.com/library/what-is-worsted-weight-yarn-a-beginners-guide/

Delia. (2019, November 12). *18 crochet projects that use just chain stitch or single crochet!* Delia Creates. https://www.deliacreates.com/17-crochet-projects-that-use-just-chain-stitch-or-single-crochet/

DIY Craftsy. (2022, April 18). *101 Free crochet patterns for beginners* (PDF to download). DIY Craftsy. https://www.diycraftsy.com/free-crochet-patterns/

Erika. (2020, July 19). *UK vs US crochet terms explained.* Don't Be Such a Square. https://www.dontbesuchasquare.com/us-vs-uk-crochet-terms-explained/

Goodale, C. (2019, July 21). *4 ways for how to seam crochet pieces together.* E'Claire Makery. https://eclairemakery.com/4-ways-for-how-to-seam-crochet-pieces-together/

Heather. (2020, August 17). *How to read crochet patterns.* The Unraveled Mitten. https://theunraveledmitten.com/2020/08/17/how-to-read-crochet-patterns/

Jackofsky, E. (2020, July 20). *Crocheting in the round: a step by step tutorial.* The Spruce Crafts. https://www.thesprucecrafts.com/crocheting-in-the-round-979084

Jamey. (2017, September 30). *The Elizabeth stitch – easy crochet tutorial.* Dabbles & Babbles. https://dabblesandbabbles.com/elizabeth-stitch-easy-crochet-tutorial/

Jamey. (2019, April 11). *20 basic crochet stitches.* Dabbles & Babbles. https://dabblesandbabbles.com/basic-crochet-stitches/

Janine. (2021, July 1). *The pros and cons of knitting vs crochet.* Craftfix. https://www.craftfix.com/knitting-vs-crochet/

Joan. (2022). *31 Half double crochet project.* Pinterest. https://za.pinterest.com/craftershaven/half-double-crochet-projects/

Johanson, M. (2019, August 13). *Popcorn crochet stitch tutorial.* The Spruce Crafts. https://www.thesprucecrafts.com/popcorn-crochet-stitch-tutorial-4688588

Johanson, M. (2020, September 27). *How to Crochet the Puff Stitch.* The Spruce Crafts. https://www.thesprucecrafts.com/how-to-crochet-the-puff-stitch-4589004

Johanson, M. (2019, October 21). *A guide to crochet hooks and how to use them.* Martha Stewart. https://www.marthastewart.com/2140269/crochet-hooks

Kelly, T. (2013, August 7). *Picot single crochet & granule stitch.* Moogly. https://www.mooglyblog.com/picot-single-crochet-granule-stitch/

Kinsler, G. B. (2020, October 10). *Gwen Blakley Kinsler LOVES yarn.* Craft Yarn Council. https://www.craftyarncouncil.com/gwen-blakley-kinsler

Knit Picks. (2022). *Free crochet patterns.* Knit Picks. https://www.knitpicks.com/crochet/free-crochet-patterns/c/301206

Langford, R. (2019, September 19). *How to know if crocheting for profit is right for you.* Yarn & Chai. https://yarnandchai.com/how-to-know-if-crocheting-for-profit-is-right-for-you/

lovecrafts. (2022). *Free crochet patterns*. lovecrafts. https://www.lovecrafts. com/en-us/l/crochet/crochet-patterns/free-crochet-patterns

Macaroni, S. (2018, January 11). *How to crochet in the round – a step-by-step picture tutorial*. Sigoni Macaroni. https://www.sigonimacaroni.com/how-to-crochet-in-the-round/

Macaroni, S. (2019, March 15). *Counting crochet stitches and rows: your beginner questions answered*. Sigoni Macaroni. https://www.sigonimacaroni.com/ counting-crochet-stitches-and-rows/

Marks, R. (1997, September). *Crochet Guild of America*. Www.crochet.org. https://www.crochet.org/page/CrochetHistory#:~:text=One%3A%20Cro chet%20originated%20in%20Arabia

McDonell-Parry, A. (2018, June 5). *The History of Macrame Is in Fact Fascinating*. Hunker. https://www.hunker.com/13712633/the-history-of-macrame-is-in-fact-fascinating

MJ. (2015, August 31). *Welcome to MJs off the hook crochet patterns!* MJ's Off the Hook Designs. https://www.mjsoffthehookdesigns.com/

Morgan, J. (2022, July 5). *Crochet facts – 30 amazing things – I bet you never knew!* Crochet Penguin. https://crochetpenguin.com/crochet-facts/

Morgan, J. (2022, January 14). *History of crochet & who invented crochet. A guide to crochet history*. Crochetpenguin.com. https://crochetpenguin.com/ history-of-crochet/

Ohrenstein, D. (2017, August 13). *Crochet origins: an enigmatic tale*. Interweave. https://www.interweave.com/article/crochet/crochet-origins-enigmatic-tale/

Piantanida, L., & Wiatr, J. (2017, December 19). *Our favorite free crochet patterns of 2021*. AllFreeCrochet. https://www.allfreecrochet.com/Miscella neous-Crochet/Our-Favorite-Free-Crochet-Patterns

Raffamusa. (2021, May 26). *How to crochet the waistcoat stitch or knit stitch – a step-by-step tutorial*. Raffamusa Designs. https://raffamusadesigns.com/ crochet-waistcoat-knit-stitch/

Red Heart, Design Team. (2022). *How to incorporate new yarns in crochet*. https://www.yarnspirations.com/how-to-join-new-yarn-in-crochet.html

Red Heart, Design Team. (2022) *The ultimate guide to left-handed crochet*. https://www.yarnspirations.com/ultimate-guide-to-left-handed-crochet.html

Fragola, S-J. (2021, April 14). *Side saddle stitch*. Bella Coco Crochet. https://bellacococrochet.com/side-saddle-stitch/

Shaimes, M. (2017, April 16). *Interesting facts about crochet you may not know.* Megmade with Love. https://megmadewithlove.com/blog-2/2017/4/12/interesting-facts-about-crochet-you-may-not-know

Sierra. (2017, May 1). *4 ways to crochet straight edges and eliminate the awful gap.* Sweet Everly B. https://sweeteverlyb.com/crochet-even-edges/

Silk, E. (2021, April 22). *The benefits of crocheting.* MueZart. https://www.muezart.com/blogs/muezart-musings/the-benefits-of-crocheting

Solovay, A. (2018, November 21). *How to treble crochet.* The Spruce Crafts. https://www.thesprucecrafts.com/how-to-treble-or-triple-stitch-4083325

Solovay, A. (2019, July 1). *How to Create Tunisian Crochet Stitches.* The Spruce Crafts. https://www.thesprucecrafts.com/tunisian-crochet-stitches-979408

Solovay, A. (2019, December 9). *How to crochet shell stitch.* The Spruce Crafts. https://www.thesprucecrafts.com/how-to-crochet-a-shell-stitch-979096

Solovay, A. (2020, April 9). *6 basic crochet stitches for beginners.* The Spruce Crafts. https://www.thesprucecrafts.com/basic-stitches-in-crochet-978516

Sylwia. (2018, March 8). *How to crochet the moss stitch.* Mycrochetory. https://mycrochetory.com/crochet-the-moss-stitch-tutorial/

Vercillo, K. (2019, June 26). *How to crochet the star stitch.* The Spruce Crafts. https://www.thesprucecrafts.com/how-to-crochet-star-stitch-4056336

Vercillo, K. (2019, July 1). *How to do half double crochet stitch (HDC).* The Spruce Crafts. https://www.thesprucecrafts.com/how-to-half-double-crochet-stitch-3576850

Vercillo, K. (2019, October 29). *29 Unique Crochet Techniques to Try.* The Spruce Crafts. https://www.thesprucecrafts.com/unique-crochet-techniques-to-try-979256

Vercillo, K. (2020, January 4). *How to crochet a double treble stitch (DTR).* The Spruce Crafts. https://www.thesprucecrafts.com/how-to-crochet-a-double-treble-stitch-978514

Vercillo, K. (2020, January 11). *How to crochet cluster stitch.* The Spruce Crafts. https://www.thesprucecrafts.com/how-to-crochet-cluster-stitch-4058572

WATG. (2015, May 13). *A brief history of crochet.* Wool and the Gang. https://www.woolandthegang.com/blog/2015/05/a-brief-history-of-crochet

West, M. et al. (2021, May 27). *Whipstitch.* WikiHow. https://www.wikihow.com/Whipstitch

Betts, J. (2022). *Crochet abbreviations: a glossary of essential terms.* Your Dictionary | Abbreviations. https://abbreviations.yourdictionary.com/articles/crochet-abbreviations.html

IMAGE REFERENCES

Chapter 1:

Delicate lace. (n.d.). [Image]. 3833463_340. https://pixabay.com/images/search/lace%20crochet/

Knitting with crochet edging. (n.d.). [Image]. 1729627_340. https://pixabay.com/images/search/lace%20crochet/

Pink crochet. (n.d.). [Image]. 2139617_340. https://pixabay.com/images/search/lace%20crochet/

Crochet essentials. (n.d.). [Image]. https://www.shutterstock.com/image-photo/knitting-sewing-supplies-458535130

Holding the yarn. (n.d.). [Image]. Julia Potapova. https://pixabay.com/photos/crochet-handmade-needlework-3608904/

Knitting. (n.d.). [Image]. 1430153_340. https://pixabay.com/images/search/knitting/

Macramé knotting. (n.d.).[Image]. 5208154_340. https://pixabay.com/images/search/macrame/

Chapter 2:

Mother and daughter. (n.d.). [Image]. @Natanavo via Twenty20. https://www.twenty20.com/photos/0c85681f-7eb8-448b-9133-252a26dcafa2/

Community hands. (n.d.). [Image]. Lola Reyes. https://pixabay.com/photos/needle-crochet-crafts-thread-1481702/

White doilie. (n.d.). [Image]. 1126825_340. https://pixabay.com/images/search/crochet/

Macramé belts. (n.d.). [Image]. 6079698_340. https://pixabay.com/images/search/macrame/

Yarn star stitch. (n.d.). [Image]. 5015883_340. https://pixabay.com/images/search/crochet/

Chapter 3:

Pattern notes. (n.d.). [Image]. Karina L. https://unsplash.com/s/photos/crochet-coasters

Crochet symbols. (n.d.). [Image]. Amy creative Designs. [Image]. https://www.etsy.com/listing/950971468/easy-crochet-charts-crochet-chart

Left-handed crochet. (n.d.). [Image]. https://pixabay.com/photos/crochet-needlework-crochet-hook-2753713/

Tunisian crochet. (n.d.). [Image]. Trudy de Roeck. https://www.twenty20.com/photos/61777e24-7ea8-4a2a-b830-e61b493ee153/

Lace crochet techniques. (n.d.). [Image]. Galina's Tales. 1156788577. https://www.shutterstock.com/catalog/licenses

Amigurumi rabbit. (n.d.). [Image]. Koy_Hipster. Royalty Free Stock Photo ID 1508352944. https://www.shutterstock.com/catalog/licenses

Bavarian headband. (n.d.). [Image]. Contributor lantapix. 17212564. https://www.shutterstock.com/catalog/licenses

Lake Constance. (n.d.). [Image]. 673103_340. https://pixabay.com/images/search/crochet/

Chapter 4:

Hook varieties. (n.d.). [Image]. Vector Contributor olnik_y. 328374983. https://www.shutterstock.com/catalog/licenses

Crochet essentials. (n.d.). [Image]. Vector Contributor casejustin. 1352818361. https://www.shutterstock.com/catalog/licenses

Crochet hooks. (n.d.). [Image]. Vector Contributor DnBr. 568248895. https://www.shutterstock.com/catalog/licenses

Crochet hook conversion chart. (n.d.). [Image]. Amy Creative Creations. https://www.etsy.com/listing/950971468/easy-crochet-charts-crochet-chart

Yarn types. (n.d.). [Image]. Contributor Astaru. 1248865561. https://www.shutterstock.com/catalog/licenses

Alpaca. (n.d.). [Image]. Elli Rader. https://www.twenty20.com/photos/b6a1d34c-c803-4880-9ad7-33a295c614d6/

Angora. (n.d.). [Image]. 44161_340. https://pixabay.com/images/search/angora/

Yarn chart. (n.d.). Amy Creative Creations. [Image]. https://www.etsy.com/market/amy%27s_creations

Hook organizer. (n.d.). [Image]. Knit pro. https://unsplash.com/photos/kN6kOIfyntk

Chapter 5:

Hand holding hook in pencil grip. (n.d.). [Image]. 1938151_340. https://pixabay.com/images/search/crochet/

Lee, F. (2022). *Slip knot steps 1-4* [Image]. From author's personal photo collection.

Lee, F. (2022). *Magic ring steps 1-7* [Image]. From author's personal photo collection.

Lee, F. (2022). *Yarn over.* [Image]. From author's personal photo collection.

Foundation chain. (n.d.). [Image]. @milola via Twenty20. https://www.twenty20.com/photos/9601e867-71b4-434b-bba6-17abed46a1be/

Slip stitch. (n.d.). [Image]. https://pixabay.com/photos/crochet-handmade-yarn-wool-thread-5164435/

Lee, F. (2022). *Single crochet.* [Image]. From author's personal photo collection.

Lee, F. (2022). *Half-double crochet.* [Image]. From author's personal photo collection.

Lee, F. (2022). *Double crochet.* [Image]. From author's personal photo collection.

Lee, F. (2022). *Treble crochet.* [Image]. From author's personal photo collection.

Joining seam. (n.d.). [Image]. Milola via Twenty20. https://www.twenty20.com/photos/9601e867-71b4-434b-bba6-17abed46a1be/

Chapter 6:

Stitch abbreviation chart. (n.d.). [Image]. Merry Meg Co. https://www.etsy.com/listing/1130168180/crochet-stitches-chart-digital-download.

Single crochet. (n.d.). [Image]. https://pixabay.com/images/search/yarn/?pagi=3&

Half-double crochet. (n.d.). [Image]. @1991mijovia Twenty20. https://www.twenty20.com/photos/11d40f37-4091-422b-b789-33fedaa7dc0f/

Double crochet granny squares. (n.d.). [Image]. Twenty20.com @limmonnaa. https://www.twenty20.com/photos/e6cf04e8-9aa7-4500-ade1-aacbc184da2b

Treble crochet baby's bonnet. (n.d.). [Image]. Annisa Ica. https://unsplash.com/s/photos/yarn

Double treble crochet. (n.d.). [Image]. https://pixabay.com/images/search/crochet/

Triple treble crochet. (n.d.). [Image]. Nykeya Paige. https://unsplash.com/s/photos/crochet-coasters

Shells. (n.d.). [Image]. Chantelle via Twenty20. https://www.twenty20.com/photos/8a32a3fc-e4b2-4632-9c2f-0afd2affd42f/

Clusters. (n.d.). [Image]. Mohadese Marvi. https://unsplash.com/s/photos/yarn

Bobbles. (n.d.). [Image]. @stevensemily36 via Twenty20. https://www.twenty20.com/photos/944ee545-160c-4435-ae74-b05f2e47aee3/

Popcorn. (white). (n.d.). [Image]. @Chantelle via Twenty20. https://www.twenty20.com/photos/c11bff8d-d159-4a39-b887-ddae2f68f71e/

Puff stitch. (n.d.). [Image]. clandia20 via Twenty20. https://www.twenty20.com/photos/783d8f60-4ae2-4689-b934-2f58eb13d51c/

Filet crochet. (n.d.). [Image]. 1129537_340. https://pixabay.com/images/search/crochet/

Granny stripe throw. (n.d.). [Image]. 1827628_340. https://pixabay.com/images/search/crochet/

Star stitch. (n.d.). [Image]. @tempramentje via Twenty20. https://www.twenty20.com/photos/4ce3b2da-3656-4a4a-93f1-7b5322ea17bf/

Cluster stitch. (n.d.). [Image]. Merylove Art. https://unsplash.com/s/photos/cluster-crochet

Waistcoat stitch. (n.d.). [Image]. 1245171_340. https://pixabay.com/images/search/crochet/

Shell stitch. (n.d.). [Image]. 2634134_340. https://pixabay.com/images/search/crochet/

Yarn crochet. (pink). (n.d.). [Image]. 334129_340. https://pixabay.com/images/search/crochet/

Crochet stitches - page 1. (n.d.). [Image]. Craftique Redux. https://www.etsy.com/listing/727003917/handy-laminated-crochet-stitches

Crochet stitches - page 2. (n.d.). [Image]. Craftique Redux. https://www.etsy.com/listing/727003917/handy-laminated-crochet-stitches

Chapter 7:

Hooks and stitch markers. (n.d.). [Image]. Objectsofinterest. https://www.twenty20.com/photos/053cd2b9-67c7-4895-9af5-eb95048d580b

Left-handed crochet. (n.d.). [Image]. @AZ.BLT via Twenty20. https://www.twenty20.com/photos/d7d524f1-5828-4999-992d-6370d9952244/

Chapter 8:

Lee, F. (2022). *Heelless socks*. [Image]. From author's personal collection.

Fingerless mittens. (n.d.). [Image]. @catanne via Twenty20. https://www.twen ty20.com/photos/1a0c736c-4d3f-49ab-8967-36fdedbacd20/

Crochet beanie. (n.d.). [Image]. Annisa Ica. https://unsplash.com/s/photos/ crochet-motifs

Trendy headbands. (n.d.). [Image]. Nikuwka. https://www.istockphoto.com/ photo/knit-winter-headbands-gm925685398-254018934

Stylish scarf. (n.d.). [Image]. Matthew Fassnacht. https://unsplash.com/s/ photos/scarf

Coaters. (n.d.) [Image]. Céline Druguet. https://unsplash.com/s/photos/ crochet

Granny square tote. (n.d.). [Image]. JOONY. https://unsplash.com/s/photos/ crochet-motifs

www.ingramcontent.com/pod-product-compliance
Lightning Source LLC
Chambersburg PA
CBHW060913120626
46553CB00001B/307